The Global Education Industry

The Global Education Industry

Lessons from Private Education in Developing Countries

JAMES TOOLEY

The Institute of Economic Affairs

First published in Great Britain in 1999 by
The Institute of Economic Affairs
2 Lord North Street
Westminster
London SW1P 3LB

This second edition with a new preface published in 2001 by
The Institute of Economic Affairs
in association with Profile Books Ltd

A CIP catalogue record for this book is available from the British Library.

ISBN 0 255 36503 9

Typeset in Stone by MacGuru
info@macguru.org.uk

Printed and bound in Great Britain by Hobbs the Printers

CONTENTS

THE AUTHOR

James Tooley is Professor of Education Policy at the University of Newcastle, England. Prior to this he was Senior Research Fellow in the School of Education, University of Manchester. He is also Director of the Education Programme at the Institute of Economic Affairs, London. Professor Tooley gained his PhD from the Institute of Education, University of London and has held research positions at the University of Oxford's Department of Educational Studies and the National Foundation for Educational Research. He has taught at Simon Fraser University (Canada), the University of the Western Cape (South Africa) and as a mathematics teacher at schools in Zimbabwe. He is a columnist for *Economic Affairs*, and is the author of *Disestablishing the School* (1995), *Education without the State* (1996), *The Higher Education Debate* (1997), *Educational Research: A Critique* (with Doug Darby, 1998), *The Global Education Industry* (1999) and *Reclaiming Education* (2000).

ACKNOWLEDGEMENTS

Without the assistance of the educational businesses featured as case studies in this paper, I could not have accomplished much. I wish to thank all those involved, the directors, chairmen, finance managers, teachers, governors and students, for their inestimable help, in allowing me or my representatives into their institutions, and giving so freely of their time, knowledge and expertise. Thanks, too, to all of the project consultants in a dozen or so countries who contributed to the study. Staff at the International Finance Corporation and World Bank also have my thanks and appreciation. In particular, I wish to thank Jack Maas, Harry Patrinos, Shobhana Sosale and, above all, Arthur Karlin, for guidance and keen interest in the project.

I also gratefully acknowledge the support from the Government of Japan, through the Comprehensive Japan Trust Fund with the IFC, for a significant amount of the funding for this study. Without this support, the research would not have been possible.

Finally, many thanks to the others on the project team, in Manchester, Kevin McNeany, Professor Tom Christie, Calvin T. Samuel and Dr Don Taylor, and in Canada, Professor E. G. West.

J . T .

FOREWORD

Education is clearly a critical area for developing countries, and has for some time been an area of focus of the development community. In the past, however, there was limited attention to the role of private education in the overall mix of educational institutions in these countries. As we at the International Finance Corporation (the private sector lending arm of the World Bank Group) have moved into new investment areas, such as infrastructure and health, we have also become aware of the potential to participate in private sector education investments. However, there was little information to guide us on the types of investment opportunities available in private education in developing countries, let alone information on how best to evaluate prospective private education projects. We therefore worked with support from education specialists at the World Bank to commission a global study of private education in developing countries. The study used detailed case studies of private education companies to draw conclusions on the key elements for successful investments in these types of companies, and examined the education sector in a number of countries to identify types of investment opportunities in private education appropriate for support by development institutions such as IFC.

The study contributors, from the University of Manchester, Nord Anglia PLC, and the Institute of Economic Affairs, provided a mix of academic and private sector perspectives that allowed them to highlight both public and private considerations of interest to IFC.

The study presented many new insights into the world of private education in developing countries, and provided a great deal of new factual material that had previously not been available. We are therefore pleased to make this information available to a wider audience through the publication of this monograph, which provides the major highlights from the study material. We hope that this material will contribute to continued growth of understanding of this very important sector.

BIRGITTA KANTOLA
Vice President, Finance and Planning
International Finance Corporation
March 1999

As with all IEA publications, the views expressed in this study are those of the author, not of the Institute (which has no corporate view), its Managing Trustees, Academic Advisory Council members or senior staff.

COLIN ROBINSON
Editorial Director, Institute of Economic Affairs
Professor of Economics, University of Surrey

PREFACE TO THE SECOND EDITION

To my surprise, this little book has proved rather popular. It was written back in 1999 as a record of a pioneering study I had the privilege of directing for the International Finance Corporation, looking at the nature and extent of private education in developing countries. The study, this book, and the various international conferences organised around it (see for example IFC, 1999) have all generated an excitement and mood which I had not really anticipated at the time. Governments and international agencies, it seems, are increasingly concerned about the wastefulness, inefficiency and lack of innovation in state education. Ideas on privatisation, public–private partnerships, voucher systems and an increasing role for the private sector are now becoming commonplace in discussions in developing countries. If this book has played some small part in that process, then this is particularly gratifying.

The occasion of this second edition enables me to write a new introduction. Given the book's status as a unique record of the particular global study, it is not the time or place to revise it extensively – even if one had the resources to revisit all of the country and company data. In any case, rewriting the book to take into account all that has been learnt about the private sector in education worldwide in the last year or two would inevitably introduce caveats and qualifications, and perhaps the text would lose some of the freshness and vitality that a first exposure to the industry prompted. Increasing complexity can be included in further publications – and a lifetime's work stretches out ahead, building on the foundation laid in this book. Research under way by myself and colleagues, to be published in due course, includes:

- further study of the regulatory environment in developing countries, culminating in the development of an Education Freedom Index, to compare countries and look for correlations between freedom and outcomes
- a conceptual, empirical and historical investigation of market versus state qualifications and accreditation
- further research exploring the nature, extent and effectiveness of private schools for the poor in India and Africa
- an exploration of a potential commercial model for using the Internet to reach the poor in India, and beyond; and
- a study of quality control and market-based management systems in the education industry.

The ideas on equity in Chapter 3 of this book have already been taken further in my *Reclaiming Education* (Tooley, 2000), which can act as a companion volume to this one, outlining the case – conceptual, philosophical, economic and social – for moving towards a greater role for the private sector in education.

In this introduction, then, I will do three things, and leave the existing text as a snapshot of the education industry at a particular moment in time. First, I will correct an impression which emerges from the text about 'private schools for the poor'. Second, I will bring up to date the record on the Indian company NIIT, which features heavily in the text, and which, being one of the most innovative of the education companies reviewed here, acts as a useful barometer for the changes and developments one is likely to see across the industry as a whole. Third, I will point briefly to developments in China, a country not covered in the text but which is clearly of some importance in any discussion of the developing world.

Private schools for the poor

In Chapter 3 on Equity Issues (p. 71 of the 1st edition, p.104 in this), I wrote:

> There are schools which cater for very low income groups in rural or urban areas, charging very low fees, and offering education of variable quality – usually with high student/ teacher ratios (up to 90 students per teacher), offering a basic education with no frills. In India, for example, these schools charge fees ranging from Rs. 50 to Rs. 150 per month and are usually sponsored by local philanthropists or by religious or minority charitable organisations.

I regret the tone of that paragraph now, and the implication that what is being offered in such schools may not be particularly valuable. My research since then, in Africa and especially in India, points to a completely different appraisal of the role of such schools. This work will be published in due course, but let me make some brief notes about such schools here, so that the misleading impression given by the above paragraph is not the lasting one taken away from this book.

Consider the private schools serving the poor in India, which I noted in that paragraph. Any visitor to the 'slums' of any of the big cities in India will be struck by the sheer number of private schools

– there seems to be one on almost every street corner, or down every alleyway. Some of these schools confusingly follow what they see as English tradition and call themselves 'public'[1] schools, but they are wholly private in every way, and are certainly not élitist institutions. Many have grouped themselves in federations, and I had the privilege to be introduced to the largest of these in Andhra Pradesh, the 'Federation of Private Schools' Management', based in Hyderabad, with 500 schools, almost 50 per cent of the total of private unaided schools in Hyderabad. Certainly the fees at these schools are low, but even 'fees ranging from Rs. 50 to Rs. 150 per month', that is, from about 75 pence (50 cents) to £2.25 ($1.50) per month, are not insignificant for the urban and rural poor in India. And government schools are available usually for free, and at many free rice is provided at lunch-time. So the key question is, why do parents prefer to send their children to these unaided and often unrecognised private schools – which itself brings disadvantages to students – when there are government schools available? Usefully, there is some recent government-sponsored research which partly provides the answers, and which makes us view the private schools in a much more favourable light – a view which has been backed up by my own research in these schools.

The *Public Report on Basic Education in India* (PROBE Team, 1999) looked at primary education in poor villages in five Indian states, both public and private, and paints a disturbing picture of the 'malfunctioning' which is taking place in *government* schools for the poor – but not, it turns out, in the private schools. The state

---

1   In England, the most élitist private schools, such as Eton, Harrow and Winchester, are called 'public schools'.

schools suffered from poor physical facilities and high pupil–teacher ratios, but what is most alarming is the low level of teaching activity taking place. When researchers called unannounced on their random sample of government schools, only in 53 per cent was there any 'teaching activity' going on (p. 47). In fully 33 per cent, the headteacher was absent. The investigators found it particularly worrying that Class 1 children seemed to be 'systematically neglected'.

Clearly poor infrastructure and apathetic parents are a problem; the overly academic imposed curricula are paralysing to teachers and students alike; teachers are burdened with excessive paperwork, and there is 'unsupportive' and inadequate management. But the deterioration of teaching standards is not just to do with disempowered teachers:

> The PROBE survey came across many instances where an element of plain negligence was . . . involved. These include several cases of irresponsible teachers keeping a school closed or non-functional for months at a time; a school where the teacher was drunk, while only one-sixth of the children enrolled were present; other drunk teachers, some of who expect pupils to bring them *daru* [drink]; a headteacher who asks the children to do domestic chores, including looking after the baby; several cases of teachers sleeping at school; . . . a headteacher who comes to school once a week; another headteacher who did not know the name of a single child in the school . . . (p. 63)

Significantly, the low level of teaching activity occurred even in those schools with relatively good infrastructure, teaching aids and pupil–teacher ratio. Even in such schools,

> Inactive teachers were found engaged in a variety of

pastimes such as sipping tea, reading comics or eating peanuts, when they were not just sitting idle. Generally, teaching activity has been reduced to a minimum, in terms of both time and effort. And this pattern is not confined to a minority of irresponsible teachers – it has become a way of life in the profession. (p. 64)

But all of these highlight the underlying problem in the public schools: the 'deep lack of accountability in the schooling system'. Crucially, these problems *were not found in the private schools* – that is, the private schools for the poor that I had rather summarily dismissed in the paragraph above. The PROBE team found a considerably higher level of teaching activity taking place in the private schools, even though the work environment was not necessarily better. In the private schools, teachers are teaching, even though they are paid significantly less than in the state schools:

This feature of private schools brings out the key role of accountability in the schooling system. In a private school, the teachers are accountable to the manager (who can fire them), and, through him or her, to the parents (who can withdraw their children). In a government school, the chain of accountability is much weaker, as teachers have a permanent job with salaries and promotions unrelated to performance. This contrast is perceived with crystal clarity by the vast majority of parents. (p. 64)

The report continues: 'As parents see it, the main advantage of private schools is that, being more accountable, they have higher levels of teaching activity. This is confirmed by the PROBE survey: in most of the private schools we visited, there was feverish classroom activity.' Moreover, when they interviewed their large sample of parents, 'Most parents stated that, if the costs of sending a child to a government and private school were the same, they would rather send their children to a private school' (p. 102).

That is, the findings of the PROBE report suggest that poor parents are willing to pay for their children to attend unaided private schools because the quality of education offered in these schools is (in fact, not only perception) higher in the private schools, in terms of the level of teaching activity, and the commitment and dedication to students.

This evidence, supporting that which I have collected as I have continued to research these schools, suggests that the implied criticism of my earlier paragraph is out of place. These schools may not have 'frills' in the sense of the luxuries that are on offer in other of the schools I described. But they are far and away superior to those provided in the state sector, and that is the relevant criterion for comparison.

NIIT – further developments

In *Reclaiming Education*, I wrote that 'some of the most fascinating insights about the possibilities and potential for private education companies I gleaned from NIIT' (Tooley, 2000, p. 107). The more I see of the 'global education industry', the more this statement is reinforced. And it seems fair to say that where NIIT leads, others tend to follow. Given that I have conducted other research on NIIT since *The Global Education Industry* was published, it might be worth mentioning three developments, as an indicator of the way progress is being made in the more innovative of the education companies.

First, NIIT has developed a new version of their flagship programme, GNIIT – the Graduate of NIIT course – called 'iGNIIT', which involves preparing graduates for the Internet and uses the

Internet to teach the course. The course features:

- a multimedia PC for every student to practise and master what he/she learns
- free Internet connection to explore the world wide web and participate in sessions which are part of the curriculum and beyond
- a computer-based training package to help the students master certain technologies that are beyond the curriculum
- Internet-based training modules to enable the students to hone their skills and test their learning acquired during the programme
- online chat with experts on various topics.

Importantly, NIIT has also linked up with Citibank to give the opportunity for all iGNIIT students to take out a seven-year study loan towards repayment of the programme fees. These loans are an extension of the 'Total Freedom Scholarship' mentioned on pp. 77–8 of the first edition (p. 113 of this edition), taking this forward on a commercially viable basis. The Citibank study loan covers up to 90 per cent of the course fee. The student can then repay the loan over the next sixty months. Significantly, the loan does not require any collateral – so it is open to students from any socio-economic background, provided that they can pass the entrance test. The theory behind this is that any student who gains an iGNIIT will be more than able to repay the loan, given the demand for young people with Internet-related skills, in India and beyond.

In fact, the NIIT/Citibank loan scheme turns out to be far from unique. I found a dozen other schemes in India, all offered by commercial banks for students in a variety of courses. Increasingly it seems that commercial banks are recognising that student loan schemes are a viable market to develop.

Secondly, NIIT is involved in some interesting developments in public–private partnership, extending the discussion on p. 79 of the first edition (pp. 115–16 of this edition). Most notably, the government of Tamil Nadu has contracted out its high-school computer curriculum to private companies, who provide the software and hardware, while the government provides an electricity supply and the classroom. These developments are being watched with great interest by the government in Andhra Pradesh too.

For the first round of the Tamil Nadu process, bidding was for 666 senior secondary schools, or just over half of the schools. One thousand bid documents were sold and 200 bids received (of which 100 bidders were technically qualified to bid and 43 contracts were awarded). NIIT was awarded the largest of these contracts, with schools allotted in 25 out of the 29 districts, a total of 371 schools altogether. Many of the classrooms have become NIIT centres, open to the school children and teachers during the day, then for use by the franchise holder in the evenings. The contracting out of curriculum areas such as this represents an important step forward in relationships between the public and private sectors, and provides an interesting model worth watching and emulating.

Finally, NIIT's cutting-edge developments in Research and Development are mentioned on p. 46 of the first edition (pp. 71–2 of this edition). NIIT has continued to develop its R&D capability, and the NIIT research department, renamed Centre for Research in Cognitive Systems (CRCS), has recently moved to a location in the prestigious Indian Institute for Information Technology (IIT) in New Delhi. Dr Sugata Mitra, Director of CRCS, considered that this would enable NIIT to have close and productive links with some of the top engineering undergraduates in the country (IIT selects 1,200 out of 400,000 applicants from across the country), and the outstanding faculty who teach and research there.

Academic collaboration and research come first in CRCS's charter, which is a very significant step for a private education company. One particular 'blue skies' project of interest in this regard is exploring the way the poor can access the Internet: the 'hole in the wall' experiment. As background, Dr Mitra experienced what many proud parents feel when he observed his children on the family computer: 'My children have easily taught themselves to access the Internet. They must be brilliant!' Just like their father, perhaps. But then he mused: 'Perhaps there's nothing special about my children, but there's something particularly *easy* about accessing the Internet?' Thus was born the 'hole in the wall' experiment.

Usefully, the NIIT headquarters borders the slum area of Kalkaji, where there are a large number of children of all ages who don't attend school. The few who do go to government schools with poor resources, and high teacher and pupil absenteeism. Dr Mitra wondered: can *these* children also learn to access the Internet without any tuition?

His research team constructed an 'Internet kiosk' in the NIIT boundary wall, with the monitor visible through a glass plate built into the wall. The PC itself was on the other side of the brick enclosure, which was connected to the NIIT's internal network. The kiosk had access to the Internet through a dedicated connection to a service provider. There was a touch pad provided instead of a mouse, which was later modified to an unbreakable joystick. The kiosk was made operational, without any announcement or instruction, in January 1999. A video camera recorded activity near the kiosk and activity was monitored from another PC on the network.

Young boys aged between six and twelve started to use the site first, and within a few minutes had established, apparently by accident, that clicking on the touch pad was of significance. Within a few hours they had learnt the significance of the pointer changing from arrow to hand-shape. Within a few days, children of both sexes had learnt to shut down the computer and how to put shortcuts on the desktop – on one day alone, some 850 shortcuts appeared! Children quickly learnt to maximise and minimise windows, to create folders and change wallpaper settings. Soon the children were visiting websites – completely without any instruction. The Disney website became especially popular, with children playing computer games and navigating stories and cartoons. Those literate in Hindi also loved to access news, horoscopes and short-story sites. Paint also became very popular, with almost all of the 80 children who came to the kiosk learning to use it – without instruction – to make pictures or to write their own names. These are children who wouldn't have access to (physical) paint and paper in their own lives. Finally, after a small intervention, a few of the children even started learning how to use Front Page Editor, making basic web pages with text and images.

One obvious danger with such an experiment was that the computer kiosk would get vandalised. Indeed, Dr Mitra was warned that he was foolish to try because vandalism would quickly destroy it. In fact, there has been no vandalism – the mouse touch pad was broken a few times, but only apparently as a side-effect of children fighting over something else. Because of its susceptibility to breakage, NIIT invented the mouse joystick, which could not be broken, even by accident.

The observations thus far indicate that underprivileged children from the slum area, without any planned instructional intervention, could achieve a remarkable level of computer literacy. The experiment suggests that language, technical skills and education are not serious barriers to accessing the Internet, and, through this, educational and entertainment CD ROMs, but instead can lead to self- and peer-education – at least for younger children. Over the age of fourteen or so, people didn't make much sense of it all: 'where's the teacher?' they would ask.

Developments in China

Finally, we turn to China, a country which was not covered in the earlier study. But given China's huge population and its particular economic and education systems, knowledge of global private education is incomplete without some mention of the Chinese picture. And China is currently at a crucial stage in its development as regards private education. From being outlawed until the mid-1980s and with virtually no private schools at all until 1989, private education has grown dramatically so that currently 54 per cent of tertiary institutions, 20 per cent of pre-schools, 9 per cent of vocational high schools, 3 per cent of middle schools and 0.4 per cent of elementary schools are in the private sector (see Table 1).

However, private institutions have grown up in the face of some uncertainty about how the Chinese authorities would react, an uncertainty which will be brought to an end in the next year or so as the government revises its law on non-government education. The initial signs are very encouraging – at the Third National Education Conference in late June 1999, Premier Zhu Rongji outlined an important role for private education, noting that 'the lib-

Table 1 **Private education in China, 1998**

	Total public and private	Private
Pre-schools	174,550	34,910
Elementary schools (years 1–6)	609,626	2,504
Middle schools (years 6–9)	77,888	2,146
Vocational high schools (years 9–12)	10,074	899
Tertiary level	2,292	1,236

Source: Official statistics provided by Professor Wu Wei, Vice Chairman, China Educational Science Association, and Ye Zhihing, Chief, Division of Educational Philosophy, National Centre for Education Development Research, Ministry of Education, Beijing, 21 July 1999.

eration of the mind should be further promoted in order to adopt a new attitude towards non-government investment. All kinds of schools as far as they meet the needs of society should be encouraged. Both public and private equally should be encouraged together' (section 2, clause 12, *Proceedings*).

This positive tone towards private education was reinforced by The International Conference on Private Schools, held in Beijing in October 1999. It was particularly of interest that the conference was organised by, among others, the Beijing Education Commission (the municipal authority responsible for education in the capital) and the National People's Congress.

The tone of the conference, particularly from the Chinese participants, was extremely favourable in its attitude towards private education. For example, summing up the conference proceedings, the vice chair of the People's Congress, Xu Jialu, stressed how private education is 'part of our great traditions'. Confucius is credited with establishing the first private school 2,500 years ago, and since then, 'with only minor setbacks', private education has proliferated and thrived. Even at the beginning of this century, he pointed out, there were more than twice as many private schools as state schools. The key question, he announced, is: 'How can we make use of this proud, historical experience?' To ensure that the experience was put to good use, he continued, the People's Congress will continue to reform the education law, to make sure that education is made 'attractive for the encouragement of the private sector, and for international investment'.

Mr Xu was not alone in expressing such sentiments. Speaker after speaker stood up to praise the role of the private sector in education, and to point out the virtues, too, of privatisation. Ma Shuping, the Deputy Director of Education of the Beijing Municipality, pointed out how private education had grown since the 'restoration period' in 1979. Hesitantly at first, private education had re-emerged as ex-teachers had held remedial classes. Then a typing school, founded in 1921 and summarily closed during the Cultural Revolution, was reopened in 1981. This event, implicitly sanctioned by the authorities, provided a signal for private education to re-emerge in Beijing. By the end of 1981, there were 28 private schools registered. The first private university was established in 1982, and by the end of the 1980s there were already 500 private schools in Beijing alone. Mr Ma pointed out that, with twenty years' experience of a burgeoning private sector, 'government's hold on education has been broken'.

Why are the Chinese authorities becoming attracted to private education? Mr Ma had five major themes, which were reiterated by other keynote speakers. First, 'to make up for a lack of government funds' – because it was recognised that the government could not cater for demand for education. Second, 'to promote educational innovation' – because it was recognised that the private sector was better at this than the state. Third, 'to ease unemployment` – because the private sector could much better respond to the market in terms of training for business and industry. Fourth, 'to stimulate education consumption' – because the private sector was better able to exploit market opportunities and make them available to a wider public. Finally, 'to help close the gap between the rich and poor' – because in China, as in many other developing countries, public educational expenditure is geared disproportionately to higher income groups and to higher education: 'If richer groups buy private education, then state resources will be available for the poor,' he commented.

But it is not just investment in private schools which is 'sincerely welcomed' by the People's Congress. State schools are also being *privatised*. There are now a dozen schools in Beijing, one in Xi'an, twenty in Shanghai and many more in other coastal cities which have been contracted out to the private sector. Perhaps the most interesting feature of the contractual arrangement is how far these are genuine privatisations. Teachers are gradually transferred to the private sector, so that the contractor is the employer of all teachers in the school within three years. This is in sharp contrast to what happens in the UK or USA, where employment of teachers is still in the hands of the local education authority under detailed national regulations. Moreover, the privatised schools in China are contracted to provide free places for a certain number of pupils from the surrounding zone, receiving a per capita funding for these pupils. But after that, the schools can be filled with *fee-paying* students.

Moreover, Lin Weiping, Director of the Municipal Committee of Education of Wenzhou – one of the fourteen open economic zones on the coast – told participants of how their public university, founded in 1984, was now being privatised, with a 60 per cent shareholding going to private investors. 'Wenzhou', he proudly said, 'has taken the lead in the market economy.' Indeed, over 45 per cent of all tertiary students were in private education. He warmly invited potential overseas investors to Wenzhou, to explore the possibilities themselves.

Only once in the conference did appearance seem to outstrip reality. In one private school visited as part of the proceedings, participants were shown around by pupils. There was an attractive fountain and pond in the grounds, with two ducks swimming merrily. A ten-year-old pupil, noting our approval, told us: 'We brought the ducks in especially for you. When you're gone we'll eat them. We Chinese are very efficient.'

JAMES TOOLEY

INTRODUCTION

Important developments are unobtrusively taking place in private education in the developing countries. They have not been sparked off, by and large, by the action of governments or international agencies. They are not much noticed or applauded in the media. But they have a potentially dramatic impact on the lives of millions world-wide. This monograph aims to give a flavour of the private education sector in developing countries – what I call the 'global education industry'. I want to show how, why and where the private education sector is flourishing and highlight impediments to its progress. From the evidence I extrapolate to suggest potential ways in which the private education sector could be harnessed and nurtured to promote equitable development.

The paper gives an impressionistic snapshot of the global education industry in a dozen or so countries. The picture discovered was surprising to the author – and I assume it will be surprising to many readers too. Far from finding that the private education sector in developing countries was relatively small and catering predominately only for the élite, I found a sector which was rather large at all levels – primary, secondary and tertiary – which was expanding rapidly, and which featured remarkable examples of innovation. In countries such as Russia and Romania, which had until recently banned private education, the sector was burgeoning – in Moscow, the same proportion of students attend private school as they do in the UK (about 7 per cent). In countries such as Colombia, 28 per cent of total enrolment in kindergarten and primary education is in the private sector, increasing to 40 per cent at secondary school level; in Argentina and Côte d'Ivoire 30 per cent and 57 per cent respectively of secondary school enrolment is in the private sector: Indonesia has 23 per cent private primary and secondary school students, and currently a massive 94 per cent of private higher education students.

Not only is the sector large in the countries studied, but it is also in places strikingly innovative. The survey identified many instances of extensive innovation, including growth of large school chains, vertically integrated education systems, application of innovative technology and teaching and learning systems, and use of distance learning. I was particularly surprised to find the importance of brand name – which many education companies were very keen to promote on billboards and in newspaper, radio and television advertising. From the study, brand name seemed to be particularly important because it helps parents and students overcome the 'information' problem. How do parents know whether they can trust the local entrepreneur who has set up school? Because he or she is the franchisee for an established educational brand name whose quality control procedures are known and respected throughout the country. In Brazil, for example, there are seven or eight large chains of private schools – several of which also run universities, and also educational television stations. The largest, Objetivo, based in São Paulo, has about 500,000 students across Brazil. Each of the chains is convinced that in order to stay ahead of its competitors, it has to invest in quality improvements and innovation in the classroom. Perhaps the most dramatic example of this technological innovation was found in the COC chain of schools. For fees of about £3,000 per annum, this provides each student with a specially devised desk with a fold-away computer terminal, networked to CD-ROM, the Internet and the teacher's 'smart-board' – which for the uninitiated, as I was before I went to Brazil, means that the student can take home a copy of all the teacher's blackboard writings on a floppy disk afterwards.

In addition, demonstrating innovation within the private sector, the research also showed how ready the supply-side is to step in when state education is perceived to be failing to deliver quality services. One example of the willingness and versatility of educational entrepreneurs comes from India, where state university computer education is in dire straits. Graduates are churned out who have learned only Fortran and Pascal, unemployable in today's computing industries. Private enterprise in the form of NIIT – the National Institute for Information Technology – provides parallel courses for those undergraduates, teaching them, for a reasonable price, current technology and providing them with valuable work placements and recruitment services. NIIT has 400 campuses around India, and is now expanding into eighteen other countries, including China, Malaysia, Indonesia, Botswana and, wait for it, the USA. Employers now explicitly state in their advertisements that they are seeking a 'GNIIT' – a Graduate of NIIT. Significantly, because it has always been constrained by the need to make a profit, NIIT is actually aware of how precious space and teaching time are, utilising both efficiently and effectively to keep costs low. Visit an NIIT centre, and you'll find all the rooms and computers constantly in use from 7 a.m. to 10 p.m., a far cry from the wastefulness which we see in western schools and universities. Perhaps most interestingly for those of us in these universities, NIIT has two research departments, one of which has fifteen full-time researchers who are employed solely to do academic research in education. Their performance indicators are papers published in research journals and conferences attended. NIIT, whose bottom line is profit, is convinced that this makes good economic sense, and that some commercially applicable ideas will emerge.

In this monograph I will build a picture of the global education industry using examples like these, giving their background and illustrating factors which make for their success, and also those which impede their development.

Background

Interest in the private education sector – in developed as well as developing countries – is motivated by three major concerns:

- the need to restrain public expenditure, in order to reduce budget deficits and external debts, and the consequent need to find alternative sources of funds for education
- doubts about state intervention in production of goods and services, and the purported benefits of privatisation, applied to the education sector; and
- the perceived threat to equity, access and social justice by private education.

First, many governments in developing countries and transition economies are under great pressure to restrain public spending. A combination of budget deficits and external debts has led to demands for reductions in public expenditure, most conspicuously as part of the Structural Adjustment Programmes favoured by the IMF and the World Bank. These circumstances have prompted many countries to look for sources other than the public purse for financing educational expansion. Advocacy of private financing (for example, World Bank, 1986) has become increasingly common, while the search for effective cost recovery and private investment in education has become widespread (Colclough, 1997; Ziderman and Albrecht, 1995).

However, this is not the only reason why interest in an increased role for the private sector in education is being explored. For, second, doubts about state involvement in the production of goods and services, and interest in the purported benefits of privatisation, have been extended to the discussion of the education sector. 'Privatisation' programmes have been increasingly adopted by governments world-wide as responses to the perceived inadequacies of publicly controlled and financed industry and services (IFC, 1995). The question is then raised to what extent the public education sector is also subject to such critique. *Can private education improve service and opportunity?* Such deliberations were first mooted in the UK by the Institute of Economic Affairs (Peacock and Wiseman, 1964; West, 1965), and are increasingly being applied to discussion of education in developing and transition economies (see for example, Bray, 1996; Cowan, 1990). The 'bureaucratic imperative', political influence and 'rent-seeking' distort educational aims, and, just as in publicly supported industries, there is inefficiency and lack of technological innovation in the public education sector (Chubb and Moe, 1990; West, 1975; Perelman, 1992). As developed and developing countries alike adapt to the global market economy, it has been suggested that 'no education system can hope to foster choice, autonomy and accountability' – the requirements for the global market – 'without first acquiring these characteristics itself' (World Bank, 1996, p. 126). Finally, there are debates about the importance of freedom and liberty in education, usually concentrated on developed countries, but nonetheless applicable to the case of developing nations too (for instance, Glenn, 1995).

In education, more than in any other sector of the economy, except perhaps health, there are, however, widespread misgivings about private sector involvement in education. It is argued, and this is my third point, that private educational opportunities exacerbate inequity. In the developed world, there is a huge corpus of academic literature criticising any moves towards 'markets' in education (for example, Gewirtz *et al.*, 1995). *A fortiori* these arguments are said to hold against the introduction of private educational opportunities in developing countries (for example, Tilak, 1997). Importantly, these academic debates have influence on government policy and public opinion in developed and developing countries, influencing the climate for, and acceptability of, private investment in education in developing countries. Hence, one of the key issues explored throughout this monograph is the ethics of private investment in education in developing countries. Is it possible to demonstrate in the context of education 'that profit and development can go hand-in-hand'? (IFC, 1996, p. 17.)

Prompted by these concerns, the International Finance Corporation (IFC), the private finance arm of the World Bank, commissioned the study 'Investment Opportunities in Private Schools and Universities in Developing Countries' in mid-1997. It had become interested in becoming active in social infrastructure areas such as health and education, based on its perception of the very important developmental benefits to be had from these sectors. However, with very limited experience and information about the private education sector in developing countries, it first undertook a small-scale study investigating the private education sector in

Kenya (Karmokolais and Maas, 1997), then commissioned the larger study, in order to analyse in depth the investment outlook for private education projects in developing countries, and to evaluate the characteristics of successful private education projects.

The study was conducted by a team of educationalists in a consortium consisting of the University of Manchester, the Institute of Economic Affairs and the education company Nord Anglia Education plc, based near Manchester. This brought together a unique combination of expertise and experience in the theory and practice of private education in developing, as well as developed, countries. The team was ably supplemented by experienced consultants based in twelve countries, who brought detailed in-country knowledge and understanding to the study.

The project team undertook eighteen case studies of education projects and twelve country studies. Table 2 on pp. 36–7 gives brief details of the case studies, while Table 3 on p. 38 provides some background information on the countries, using mainly standardised information from earlier published sources. The countries and case studies were chosen on the basis of extensive discussions at the IFC and World Bank. The case studies were selected to cover the full range of primary, secondary, tertiary and distance learning projects. Roughly half the case studies were of for-profit education companies or schools, the other half not-for-profit foundations. Many of the educational project case studies were in countries featuring as country studies.

This monograph reports on some of the findings from this study (IFC, 1998), with four aims:

First, the major aim is to present a 'snapshot' of the private education sector in developing countries, arising from the IFC study, to inform those who know very little about this burgeoning area –

and I suspect that this will cover most readers. This aim is covered, first, in Chapter 1 by giving some brief background details of the case studies in the study, and by giving in schematic form a 'profile of a viable education company or institution', based on the research. In this section, I particularly highlight the large education companies – a novel finding of the study, I believe – and point to ways in which they may overcome some of the objections to private education. I continue, in Chapter 2, by discussing some of the factors which seem to underpin the viability of these private education projects.

Second, what is perhaps the most common objection to private education is addressed, viz., that it caters primarily for the élite, and hence has no place in the discussion of equitable development (or, indeed, extending access in developed countries). It is argued in Chapter 3 that this common conception may in fact be a misconception. The considerations there include the inequity of public provision, the hidden costs of state education, and a discussion of the way some private education companies respond to the needs of the disadvantaged by provision of innovative social responsibility programmes, subsidised places and student loan schemes.

Third, in Chapter 4, I aim to show the nature and extent of the private education sector in the countries studied in the IFC survey, and to point out some of the factors which impede or facilitate the development of the private education sector at the macro or country level. In particular, I focus on the nature and extent of the regulatory regimes which may impinge upon private education.

Finally, I consider ways in which the existence of this vibrant, innovative private sector could influence education policy – as practised by international agencies and national governments. In

Chapter 5 I spell out a 'modest' policy proposal arising from the argument, pointing to ways in which the private education sector – and in particular, the larger companies – could play an important role in promoting equitable development.

Table 2 Case studies

Name	Type of education	No. of students	Annual fees ($)	For profit?	Ownership	Leasing vs. ownership	Loan financing	Foreign exhange loans
Argentina								
Universidad de Belgrano	University	16,495	2,693–6,000	No	Foundation	Both	Yes	No
Brazil								
COC	K to pre-U	26,000	3,600–5,400	Yes	Sole prop.	Own	No	No
Objetivo/UNIP[a]	K to U	514,000	4,100–12,500	Yes	Sole prop.	Both	No	No
Pitagorás	K to pre-U	81,000	3,200–4,500	Yes	Prop.	Own	No	No
Radial Schools[a]	K to U	8,500	1,750–3,875	No	Foundation	Own	No	No
Colombia								
Univ.de Los Andes Federacion Nacional	University Schools chain	7,503 *	3,650–9,550 *	No No	Foundation Foundation	Both Own	No No	No No
India								
Delhi Public Schools Society**	Schools chain	50,000	200–420	No	Society	Own	Yes	Yes
NIIT**	Computer literacy	140,000	650	Yes	Listed company	Lease	Yes	Yes
Indonesia								
Trisakti University	University	27,481	12,170–28,695 rup***	No	Foundation	Own	Yes	Yes

K = Kindergarten; U = University; HS = High School

Table 2 (cont'd)								
Peru TESCUP**	Technical college	1,218	227–342	No	Foundation	Own	Yes	No
Romania CODECS**	Distance education	2,208	500–4,000	Yes	Joint stock co.	Lease	No	No
Russia MEPU	University	3,093	330–833	No	Foundation	Both	No	No
South Africa EDUCOR**	HS to U Prof & voc	300,000	65–1,830	Yes	Listed company	Both	No	No
Damelin Franchise	Prof & voc	373	65–1,500	Yes	Sole prop.	Lease	No	No
Thailand New International	HS	878	2,750–5,200	No	Foundation	Lease	No	No
Turkey Koç University	University	916	5,650–13,500	No	Foundation	Own	Yes	Yes
USA Sabis Ed. Systems Inc.**	K to pre-University	11,000	1,400–6,750	Yes	Incorporated company	Own	*	*
Zimbabwe Speciss College**	US to U; prof & voc	15,776	120–1,536	Yes	Limited company	Both	No	Yes

* Unavailable   ** Chains of Schools   *** Left in local currency because of extreme currency fluctuations

Table 3 Country comparison table

	Total population 1995 (million)	Population growth rate (% pa)	Adult literacy % (15+)	Gross enrolment ratio			Private secondary enrolment (% of total)	Private university enrolment (% of total)	Exchange rate, March 1996 ($1=)
				Primary	Secondary	Tertiary			
Argentina	35	1.3	96	107	73	32	30	17	0.99 peso
Brazil	159	1.5	83	99	34	12	19[a]	58	1.13 real
Colombia	37	1.8	91	119	63	10	40	60	1343.15 cp
Côte d' Ivoire	14	3.1	40	69	25	n/a	27	n/a	608.9CFA fr
India	929	1.8	52	102	n/a	n/a	42[b]	59	39.35 Rs
Indonesia	193	1.6	84	114	43	10	54	94	8850 Rp
Peru	4	5.7	87	95	53	19	7	30	0.71 dinar
Romania	23	-0.4	n/a	86	82	12	0	n/a	8090 lei
Russia	148	0.0	n/a	107	88	45	<1	n/a	n/a
South Africa	42	2.2	82	110	78	13	2	n/a	4.94 rand
Thailand	58	0.9	84	97	37	19	10	18	42.10 baht
Turkey	61	1.7	82	103	61	16	3	n/a	230875 lira

Sources: *Higher Education: The Lessons of Experience* (World Bank, 1994); *World Bank Development Report 1997* (World Bank); *World Education Report 1995* (UNESCO); IFC (1998). n/a: figures not available. [a] In São Paolo state. [b] Middle Schools including aided schools.

1 CASE STUDIES OF PRIVATE EDUCATION

When people think of private education in developing countries they usually have in mind high quality, expensive private schools catering predominantly for the children of the élite. The IFC study (IFC, 1998) revealed a completely different picture.

The study undertook case studies of eighteen[1] education projects – companies, schools and/or universities – in twelve developing countries as shown in Table 2 above. This chapter uses information from all eighteen of these studies. However, of particular interest in this monograph – and, I suggest, of particular novelty to readers – are the twelve companies with 'chains' of schools and/or colleges marked in the table. The 'potted histories' and backgrounds to these companies are grouped together at the beginning of the next section, followed by the stand-alone universities and schools. The education *companies* are particularly highlighted because they seem to offer the most interesting and dramatic potential for development and for extending access. They also, interestingly, seem to have the potential to overcome some of the common objections to private education (over and above those concerning its élitist nature, discussed in Chapter 3 below), viz., that:

---

1   It also undertook one case study in the USA, of Sabis Educational Systems Inc. Two of the eighteen case studies were of the same education company, Educor – one looking at head office, the other at a small franchise; these are reported under one heading below.

- Consumers of education suffer from the 'information' problem, allowing devious business people to take advantage of their ignorance (Barr, 1993)
- The private sector could not engage in the requisite research and development and quality control to raise standards, which needs the resources of government; hence any role for the private sector in education will inevitably be limited (Molnar, 1996).

On the contrary, with the larger education companies it is clear that the brand name works as it does for other consumer goods and services, reassuring parents and students that high quality is being offered and maintained. Molnar's (1996) particular criticism is with charter school management companies in the US, but it would seem his criticisms could be applicable more generally. He condemns what he calls 'store-front' charter schools run by

> quick-buck operators . . . Attracted by the lack of
> regulations, effective fiscal controls, or academic standards
> and untroubled by any concern for the welfare of their
> students, they will be free to set up and close down over and
> over again, milking the system for as much as they can get
> (p. 166).

But if the operators are like the chains of schools found in many developing countries, then they cannot afford to act in this way – because if the brand name is undermined, then the company will go out of business. Just as the author knows nothing about computers, but confidently purchased his current lap-top aware that the need to maintain the high quality of the brand name will keep the producers 'on their toes', so educational consumers attending, say, an Objetivo School in Brazil or an NIIT centre in India are confident that they know strict quality procedures are in place to keep quality consistently high.

Moreover, it is clear that these companies *are* able to marshal the resources required for research and development, as will be illustrated – and indeed, they have become involved in R&D often precisely because of the perceived failures of the state system within the countries to maintain high standards.

The education companies also seem to have two other important advantages if we are considering potential ways in which developed countries can aid equitable development, or, indeed, if we are considering ways in which we can extend access in developed countries. It might be feared, for example, that the least risky investments for an international investor such as the International Finance Corporation would be those high-fee schools in certain countries catering only to the élite – because only these would have sophisticated enough management and financial systems in place. But then this would be likely to open such an organisation to criticism, as it may be hard to argue that investment in these types of schools would aid development. However, I suggest that in many developing countries the 'least risky' ventures are likely to be the *big education companies*, such as Educor, South Africa; NIIT, India; TECSUP, Peru; COC, Objetivo/UNIP, Pitágoras and Radial, Brazil and Speciss College, Zimbabwe. But these institutions serve not only the élite, but a wide range of socio-economic groups. Moreover, if further aspects of the model developed in Chapter 5 below are followed, such as investment in franchise funding or the creation of a student loan company, it would seem that a low risk venture could simultaneously help develop entrepreneurial talent in the indigenous populations, with all its concomitant developmental benefits, as well as reaching out to areas currently less well-served by quality educational opportunities.

A second fear might be that if an international investor were to fund a school which should subsequently fail, then it would be politically impossible for the investor to seek to repossess its assets, given the resulting accusation that it was 'denying children their education'. In the context of the global findings, however, the intriguing possibility presents itself that, should an overseas-funded project fail, there could always be a *competing brand name* willing to take over the school or institution and seek to run it more effectively! Hence, this potentially embarrassing difficulty for overseas investors could be neatly avoided in countries where strong competition between brands exists, such as Brazil, India and South Africa, or where such competition could be encouraged. Indeed, a similar conclusion could be drawn concerning the permissibility of a private education company taking over failing state schools in, say, Britain or America.

Hence, harnessing the entrepreneurial talent and educational expertise of the education companies seems to offer a challenging and exciting way forward for educational development, as we shall explore below.

What are these private education companies like? In this chapter we give brief potted histories of each of the companies featured as case studies in the research, together with the stand-alone schools and universities for the sake of completeness.[2] We show

---

2   It is worth pointing out that the aim in the study was not to select a *representative* sample of schools or universities, but to find a range of projects, in order to give as full a 'snapshot' of the global education industry as possible. Opportunism came into it too, as companies were pointed out to us which would be worthwhile investigating, and others came up while we were travelling. It must

their origins and the motivations of the entrepreneurs who established the businesses. In the following chapter we summarise major features which related to their success, concerning research and development, the way they respond to 'the technological imperative', the importance of brand name and certification, how they have expanded and raised capital for that expansion, and, perhaps most significantly, their quality control procedures. We also look at the issues of donations and endowments, for-profit versus not-for-profit, and the management of the risk of non-payment of tuition fees.

However, rather than throw readers in at the deep end, I begin by providing a schematic summary of the factors which, from the study, I suggest will make for a successful[3] institution or

---

also be noted that much of the information obtained from the education companies was proprietary, given to the project team in confidence for the express purpose of informing the IFC about the potential for investment. Such details have of course been omitted from this paper, although they inform the context of the writer's policy proposals.

3   Let me be clear about the limitations of what we mean by 'successful' in this model. The IFC was particularly concerned to know if there were private educational opportunities in developing countries which satisfied the following criteria: (1) they are profitable (or make a surplus); (2) they are financed totally (or almost totally) from student fee income; (3) they charge comparatively modest fees, and hence are accessible to many socio-economic groups, not just the élite.

Only if these three conditions were satisfied would the IFC be likely to consider investing in private education. The study then set out to find such kinds of institutions, and all the chains of companies reported here fitted into this model, as well as the stand-alone schools and universities. The criteria for viability were the extent to which they met the above conditions. Hence, *all* of the companies described here satisfied the condition of profitability, and so passed the quality test as far as the *market* was concerned. They were able to attract customers, and, as we shall see below, to ensure that their customers were satisfied in terms of the quality of the education delivered, and that the courses led to satisfactory outcomes, in particular in terms of employment prospects. We can say that all of the companies and institutions were *successful* in these senses. However, the study

company, to give a framework in which to view the ensuing discussion.

Given the diversity of companies and institutions examined, across the whole range of education sectors, and in a variety of geographical and political contexts, it is, of course, difficult to pick out the factors that contribute to their success. Perhaps the safest course would be to eschew such generalisation altogether. However, a few pointers can be made which draw on the discussion in this and the next chapter, given in the spirit of tentative suggestions to this end.

Profile of a viable institution and/or company

For education businesses, whether stand-alone universities or vocational institutions, or chains of schools and universities, the following factors are likely to be significant for success. We can divide these factors, roughly, into those concerned with profitability, educational efficacy, and equity, as follows:

Profitability

In terms of *maintaining or increasing market share*, an education business is likely to:

---

did not set out to evaluate the effectiveness of the schools or universities in terms of their academic excellence, or relative excellence vis-à-vis the state sector, and no suggestions are made to that effect here. Nor, because we used a case study methodology, are we able to point out which of the factors described below were the most important in leading to success. Both of these issues, important as they are, will have to await further research. This study itself set out to describe a sector which research did not seem to have uncovered before. That is its importance, but the questions the study was able to answer were limited because of its novelty.

1. be concerned with promoting its brand name, perhaps spending about 10 per cent of turnover on this, and using a variety of methods. Stand-alone high schools and universities will not find this as important as chains of schools and universities

2. seek to be innovative, particularly in terms of technology in order to keep and attract customers

3. seek to expand into local, regional and sometimes international markets, and to benefit by integrating horizontally (by taking over other schools), laterally (moving into new areas of education or into recruitment, television and radio) or vertically (by moving into publishing and software development)

4. use franchising for this expansion, either through collecting royalties, or selling their pedagogical materials, to allow for expansion. Franchising is less likely to occur, however, at the university level.

In terms of *funding and management,* successful educational businesses are also likely to:

5. carefully manage the risks of non-payment of tuition fees, by employing a variety of techniques of incentives and punishment. Even in successful companies, however, bad debt is likely to run at 5 per cent of turnover

6. deploy successful management, with clear lines of authority, clearly defined roles, particularly for executive and non-executive directors, and using sophisticated information systems

7. ensure that all resources, including space, teachers and

technology, are used efficiently, perhaps going to considerable lengths to ensure this

8. seek to employ innovative technology, in order to reduce costs

9. employ dedicated researchers to consider more efficient ways of using existing resources, in order to compete efficiently and effectively deploy innovative technology

10. have had only very modest start-up capital, and to have funded all their expansion through self-generated cash flow. However, given more favourable banking circumstances (such as lower interest rates, lower collateral needed, and more sympathetic banks), they may be, or have been, keen to take out loans for investment and expansion.

Educational efficacy

In terms of *educational quality*, the successful education business is likely to:

11. use recognised certification, and to have vocational certificates endorsed by relevant professional bodies. However, when institutions have a very strong brand name, they can use their own certification, although they may persist with such endorsements or other recognised certification

12. be very concerned with quality control, particularly for those which have developed chains of operations

13. seek to employ innovative technology, in order to enhance the learning process.

Equity and social justice

A successful education business, in terms of profitability and educational efficacy, which is also concerned with equitable access can also:

14. organise its own student loan scheme, which could be financed through donations, but which is likely to be self-financing in the medium term
15. cross-subsidise some of its student places, courses or campuses, in order to allow those on lower incomes to be subsidised by those on higher incomes, or financed by business
16. seek good relations with the public education sector, in part because this is politically expedient, but also because government is likely to seek the private sector's help in improving standards within the public sector
17. have a social responsibility programme, helping the local or national community while at the same time doing much to promote the image of the company.

Irrelevancies

Finally, it seems to be *irrelevant* for a successful company or institution whether or not it:

18. has endowments or donations – although it *may* be that donations can undermine a company's incentives to innovate and work efficiently
19. is for-profit or not-for-profit
20. owns or leases property – this very much depends on local circumstances.

Given these twenty factors, we now turn to brief potted histories of the education companies explored in the IFC research.

Background and histories 1: Education companies

All but one of the education companies studied (viz., TECSUP, Peru) have relied entirely on fee income or other generated income to fund their initial growth and expansion, rather than requiring endowments or donations. TECSUP did need donations at first, but is now in a position where it can finance itself totally through fee income.

Brazil – Objetivo/UNIP

There are several chains of private schools and universities in Brazil, the largest of which is Objetivo/UNIP, with headquarters in São Paulo. (Objetivo is the school chain, UNIP the university.) The company story began in the early 1960s, when Mr João Carlos Di Genio started a coaching class for university entrance with about 20 private students. Finding considerable demand for his teaching methods, he founded an intensive cramming course in 1965 with three friends, for students to get into university. They called this course 'Objetivo'. In 1967, they utilised internal television broadcasting for their lessons – a revolutionary development at the time. Three years later they added a school, from primary to Second Grade, extended in 1974 to offer courses up to university entrance. In 1988 they were granted the title of university for their upper levels – after what they saw as a fourteen-year struggle to get such recognition.

Since then, they have continued to expand, so that now they

have approximately 500,000 students in centres and 450 franchises across Brazil, with annual turnover approximately US$400 million. School students range from pre-school and primary, through First Grade (age 11–14 years), Second Grade (15–17 years), to prep (university entrance, eighteen years). The university offers courses including business administration, teacher training, engineering, dentistry and veterinary science.

Brazil – COC

COC is perhaps the most technologically innovative of the chains of schools in Brazil. Based in Ribeirão Preto, the Director is Dr Chaim Zaher, who is the joint owner of the company, with his wife. COC has three wholly-owned schools, catering to children from kindergarten to university entrance examination. It also has 63 franchises, with the aim to increase this to 200 by year 2001. In all, there are 26,000 students in COC schools. The turnover of the company in 1997 was US$30 million. It is currently seeking to expand by opening a new university in Ribeirão Preto, introducing its technological innovation at this level to cater for a growing market.

The current owner of COC, Dr Zaher, opened a cramming college for the 'vestibular' – the Brazilian university entrance examination – in Araçatuba in 1970. This was named THATHI College (an acronym of the first initials of his daughters' names). He expanded this to open a high school five years later. Meanwhile, in 1963, a group of students from one of the best medical schools in Brazil, based in Ribeirão Preto, set up a similar cramming course. They named the course after Oswaldo Cruz, a famous Brazilian scientist. Originally the 'Curso Oswaldo Cruz' – the Oswaldo Cruz course – they changed the name later to Colegio Oswaldo Cruz, abbreviated COC. In 1972, following the success of the cramming college, a high school was added, followed in 1979 by the primary and junior high schools. In 1985, spurred on by the success of his own school, Dr Zaher bought COC from the original founders. Finally, in 1997, COC bought Escola Morumbi – one of the most highly respected private schools in São Paulo, now called Escola COC Morumbi.

Brazil – Pitágoras Group

The Pitágoras Group is a chain of schools with 80,000 students, ranging from kindergarten to pre-Vestibular as well as professional courses and adult education courses. Its headquarters is in Belo Horizonte, Minas Gerais, and it is known throughout Brazil and internationally for its concern with Total Quality Management in education. It also sponsors educational television programmes. The current school network extends over nine Brazilian states: Minas Gerais, Amazonas, Pará, Rondônia, Goiás, Maranhâo, Bahia, Espírito Santo and Paraná.

On 11 April 1966, in a Catholic college in Belo Horizonte, five young teachers held a pre-university crammer class for 35 students. Evando Neiva, now the president of Pitágoras, was the physics teacher. The fact that 33 of the 35 students passed the university entrance examination seems to have been noticed, for in the second semester of 1966, 180 students took part in these classes; by 1969, the number had grown to 1,200, with students in three shifts. In 1970, Pitágoras formed an alliance with three of the big Catholic colleges in Belo Horizonte, taking responsibility for the teaching of their university entrance courses. Inspired by its initial success here, Pitágoras decided to diversify further, and opened its own First and Second Grade schools in late 1971. To do this, it invested its own funds in the construction of a purpose-built school, Colegio Pitágoras, in a prime area of Belo Horizonte. The company was granted a two-year probationary period by the State Council of Education in 1972. To distinguish itself from other schools in Minas Gerais, the company designed a new curriculum and teaching model. By this time, 5,000 young people between eleven and eighteen were enrolled with Pitágoras, doing pre-Vestibular, First and Second Grade, and also free week-long courses as part of their social responsibility programme. In 1973 professional technical education was added to this list.

In 1994, the Pitágoras Network (Rede Pitágoras) was established, linking other schools within their quality control programme. Through this project, in 1995, Pitágoras linked in with another business, O Groupo Educare, which had First and Second Grade schools; in less than a year, the network moved up to 106 schools, and the figure now stands at 120 schools, with the expectation that this will reach 400 by the year 2000.

Brazil – Radial

Radial is a small not-for-profit educational chain based in São Paulo. It has five campuses, and covers the age-range from kindergarten to post-compulsory professional and university courses. In total, it has about 8,500 students. It is distinctive in the Brazilian environment in that it avowedly attempts to give all high school students the benefit of a vocationally relevant curriculum, as well as focusing on artistic and cultural development. Its turnover in 1997 was US$17m.

The founder of Radial was Professor Ibrahim David Curi Neto. In 1962, Professor Ibrahim founded Colégio Rui Barbosa de Admissão, in São Paulo, providing secretarial courses for 200 students. In 1965, Professor Ibrahim left the college under the directorship of his brother, and started a new technical school, in Jabaquara. In 1970 he acquired Colégio Caramuru with 80 students, catering for kindergarten through to high school. In 1975, he provided technical courses in a state school at the request of parents .

Radial School was opened in 1976, in Santo Amaro, with 600 students following courses in electronics and data processing in evening classes. By 1979, Radial had a total of 5,000 students. Next Caramuru School was merged with one of the Radial colleges, providing an integrated school, from kindergarten to post-compulsory practical and technical classes, and incorporating the combined academic and technical aspects in the curriculum throughout. This school was aimed at giving young people a high school education *combined* with vocational training. In 1989, Radial opened its first university, and in 1995, Radial was renamed IREP (Instituto Radial de Ensino e Pesquisa – Radial Institute of Teaching and Research).

Colombia – education programme of the Federacion Nacional de Cafeteros

The Federacion, created in 1927, is a not-for-profit entity, currently representing more than 80 per cent of the country's coffee cultivators, and active in scientific research, health and education. In the 1970s, the Federacion recognised the enormous educational needs in the rural areas. Noting that the rigidity of the educational system was not well suited to Colombian rural society, it created a new education model, the Escuela Nueva ('New School', hereafter EN), after extensive curriculum research and development and teacher preparation. It then began creating EN schools, constructing more than 1,100 schools in the Caldas department of Colombia, and 4,000 in the rest of the country. The Federacion develops these schools with a public or private partner; generally, the regional education departments contribute about 30 per cent of total investment. The Federacion does not see itself in competition with the public bodies, but as acting in concert with them, to provide and support the education of the rural poor. Students pay US$1 a month as fees to attend school.

The programme has established that a research-based curriculum and organisational model for schools is appropriate in meeting the educational needs of the rural poor. It has also shown the usefulness of public–private partnerships, which utilise the management expertise and finances of the private sector, together with educational expertise and some finance from the public sector. Such is the success of the project that a pilot project to extend the EN model and methodology to other Latin American and Caribbean countries is envisaged. The replicability of the model, however, would depend on finding an equivalent private company willing to donate considerable funds and governments willing to hand over management of public finances to the private sector.

India – Delhi Public Schools (DPS)

The Delhi Public School Society is a highly successful chain of private schools in India, with annual turnover of approximately US$4 million. It prides itself on excellent academic results and comparatively low fees. It has exhibited dynamic growth, particularly over the past six years, with each of the Society's core schools posting reasonable surpluses every year.

The first school, DPS–Mathura Road, was established in tents, in 1949, by a group of Indians displaced after Partition. As the fledgling school grew, the tents gave way to a permanent building, and then to the establishment of other 'core' schools in and around Delhi, and then in partnerships with state governments elsewhere. Today, there are 42 schools, with a total student population of around 50,000, and DPS is seeking 150 schools by 2001.

There are *four* types of schools, including five *core schools*, wholly owned by the Society; 32 *Satellite Schools*, located in eleven states, which have been set up and are owned by respective public sector (government) undertakings (PSUs), run on their behalf by the Society; three *Village Schools*, located in Mewat, a backward area not far from New Delhi, subsidised using surplus resources of the larger core schools; and two *overseas schools*. In addition to its schools, the DPS runs, funded from core schools surpluses: an educational think-tank and R & D centre, set up in 1993, to undertake educational research on the development of innovative teaching techniques, contemporary teaching–learning aids and courseware; and a teachers' training college, located in Delhi, offering initial and in-service teacher training – for teachers inside *and* outside the DPS system.

India – NIIT[4]

NIIT is the largest provider of computer education and training in

---

4   See also Mitra (1998).

India, with a market share of 37 per cent, annual turnover of US$73 million and profits of US$13 million. The company has more than 400 centres in India, and has recently expanded into overseas markets. It also provides training and software consultancy for companies, and has its own educational multimedia software production facility employing 550 personnel, making it the largest in the world. With a history stretching back eighteen years, NIIT boasts 500,000 alumni and a corporate network of over 1,000 companies.

NIIT was conceived in 1979 by Rajendra S. Pawar, now Vice Chairman and Managing Director, then a development officer for a computer company in Bombay. He was aware both of the need for trained computer staff and of the unsatisfactory nature of the computer education in Indian universities. With two colleagues he set up a company, which opened its first computer education centre in a leased room in an office building in downtown Bombay, in 1982. In the same year it opened a second centre in Delhi. Having achieved significant growth, in 1993 the company was listed on the Bombay and Delhi (National) Stock Exchanges. In February 1996 it opened its first education centre outside India, in Kathmandu, Nepal.

There are *four* strands to NIIT's business, the most important part being the Career Education Group (CEG). Sixty per cent of NIIT's education and training turnover comes from this. The majority – 80 per cent – of students on this course are already 'full-time' students at an Indian university. Many students and employers find Indian university computer courses unsatisfactory, because they use out of date technology and methods, and are undemanding for students. Hence NIIT works in tandem with the formal sector, and offers students a four semester (that is, two year) course to students already enrolled in a state university. Allowing time for revising for exams for both courses, at the end of three years students can become graduates of an Indian university, and have an NIIT Professional Diploma in Network-Centred Computing. The great majority also go on to the one year NIIT Professional Practice option. This is a one year placement whereby students are given a mentor in NIIT and a supervisor in the company where they are employed, and paid a stipend for their full-time work. This stipend is calculated to cover *all the fees for the two year NIIT course*. This is an extremely successful model, with over 1,000 companies taking part, and in the great majority of cases, students find full-time employment with their placement company. At the end of this process, provided they have satisfied their supervisor and mentor, they become a Graduate of NIIT (GNIIT).

Peru – TECSUP

TECSUP is a private, not-for-profit technological institute, set at the non-university 'superior' level in the Peruvian education system, with an annual turnover of approximately US$7 million. It gives young people training as applied engineers, and also offers short courses for people already working in industry. Its first centre, in Lima, opened in 1984, and the second one, in Arequipa, in 1993. Luis Hochschild, a successful Peruvian businessman, came up with the idea behind TECSUP in 1980, and, with aid from the German State of Baden-Württemberg – which donated machinery and expertise – was able to set up the Lima campus in 1984. In total, Baden-Württemberg has donated US$5 million during the period that TECSUP has been in operation. Two major types of courses offered at TECSUP are: the *core programme*, for the training of technicians, aimed at school leavers with a high level of schooling; and the *continuous education programme* which offers short courses for people already in employment, to bring them up to date with the latest technology and to develop their management skills.

The three year *core programme* leads to the 'Technical Professional Diploma' – a government diploma. In the *continuous education programme*, short courses cater for the range of technical and managerial needs of employees already in employment. Half of the short course programmes are taught *in situ* in the companies. As an additional part of this programme, TECSUP is now offering a distance learning modular MBA, in conjunction with the Universidad Politecnica de Madrid, Spain. TECSUP is also innovating into new and profitable areas for its short course programme, including distance education, and long distance video conferencing and education, and satellite courses.

South Africa – Educor

The Education Investment Corporation Limited (Educor) is the largest private education group in southern Africa – with a combined enrolment of 300,000 students on more than 40 campuses and in distance education, and with an estimated 100,000 students graduating in 1997. Its annual turnover last year was approximately US$26 million, with profits of US$6 million. Its education business covers the range from adult basic education and training (ABET), through primary, secondary and tertiary education, to postgraduate and corporate training. The Educor group comprises six main education subsidiaries: Damelin Education Group,

Midrand Campus, Eden College, the Graduate Institute of Management and Technology, INTEC, the Charter Group, and two recruitment and placement divisions – Renwick Group, and PAG Placements. The oldest of these, and the core on which the fortunes of the company has been built, is Damelin, which is itself a group of companies.

Damelin had its roots in Damelin College, which was founded in 1943 by Dr Benjamin Damelin as a cramming college. Johann Brummer joined as a teacher in 1951, became a partner in 1952, and today is Executive Chairman of Educor. A key step in the development of the brand name was in 1952, when Johann Brummer started developing distance learning materials, which became Damelin Correspondence College, founded in 1955. Brummer was aware that the majority of African teachers in rural areas had not graduated from high school, and he sought to improve their conditions with a programme of high school graduation through distance learning. He also saw an untapped and potentially lucrative market.

In the early 1960s, Damelin started offering evening classes from the Johannesburg site – this was the start of the Damelin Campus, which now offers business and degree courses. Next, in 1968, came the Damelin Management School, offering specific training for adults, towards Damelin certificates endorsed by the professional institutes. Finally, in the early 1980s, Damelin Computer School was started, initially only offering part-time courses. Educor was formed in 1996 when the Housewares Group bought Damelin and Midrand College. In June 1996, Educor was listed on the Johannesburg Stock Exchange.

Romania – CODECS

CODECS – the Centre for Open Distance Education for Civil Society – is a distance learning institution, based in Bucharest, with twelve regional centres throughout Romania. It provides the UK's Open University Business School courses in business management, as well as specialised consultancy and short courses. It has been in business for five years, and now has over 2,500 students on its books. Turnover in 1996 was US$660,000.

In 1992, the Open University Business School (OUBS), UK, organised a programme in Romania, financed by the British Know How Fund. After graduation, the first 24 students, trained in competitive management, decided to found their own distance learning company. With an initial capital of only US$325, CODECS was established in 1993. It now has over 2,500 students on its books and has more applicants than it can cater for, running a waiting list.

CODECS was registered as a joint-stock company, a position which remains the same today. It is a for-profit company: although Romanian education law stipulates that private education must be organised and function on non-profit principles, the same law allows institutions *including commercial companies* to deliver professional training programmes of adults through distance learning.

CODECS functions on a licence contract with the Open University. Formally the students enrolled are also registered as OUBS students, hence they are considered to be Romanian students enrolled in a foreign university. In 1995 CODECS received functioning approval from the Ministry of National Education, although the diplomas issued by CODECS are not yet endorsed by the Ministry.

Zimbabwe – Speciss College

Speciss College is the largest, most diverse and most comprehensive provider of quality training and education in Zimbabwe, providing high school, professional training, tertiary education, in-employment/job related training and remedial education for people with educational or learning problems. Annual turnover is approximately US$3 million.

In 1965, George Laverdos met the principal of the International Correspondence College in Salisbury, Rhodesia, David Sutherland. Laverdos had been teaching a 'How to Study' course in Greece and Sutherland asked him to spend two weeks writing a similar course for the Rhodesian market. When the course was written, it was suggested that Laverdos should stay behind and teach the course; after leafleting outside several of the major city schools, they had applicants enough for six classes of twelve students. Buoyed by this success, they set up a cramming college, the National Coaching Academy (NCA), modelled explicitly on Damelin High School, but internal disagreements prompted Laverdos to move to Bulawayo, where he started a 'how-to-study' course, which evolved into Speciss College in Bulawayo. (SPECISS is the acronym of Laverdos' study method, *State, Preview, Explore, Comprehend, Involve, Systematise, Summarise*.) After four years, Laverdos brought his concept to Salisbury, and NCA and Speciss merged under the latter's name. They then bought out Lobengula College (in a township of Bulawayo) and Magaba College (in the township of Harare – now Mbare – in the capital) from their owners. Laverdos' motivation for all the work is quite explicit – to tap into new markets, for purely financial considerations. This was particularly true of his taking over the African colleges in Magaba and Lobengula. He was driven by business opportunism, to address a market – black and lower income level – which was not being catered for.

Since independence in 1980, Speciss has diversified into computers and print and mail companies, and bought the Athol Desmond College – a private college offering remedial and language enrichment classes. Under Speciss it strengthened its psychological testing and careers advice. Speciss now has approximately 30,000 students across these five campuses.

Background and histories 2: Stand-alone schools and universities

We now turn to the stand-alone schools and universities which were part of the IFC study. Many of the features found in the education companies will be found in these examples, in particular, the way in which the majority of them are funded almost entirely through fee income.

Argentina – Universidad de Belgrano

In 34 years, the Universidad de Belgrano (UB) has grown from a 90-student, 28-professor operation in a rented building, to a university with 16,495 students and 2,470 professors. Today the UB has 12 faculties, two schools in 28 buildings throughout Buenos Aires. In all, some 24,000 students have graduated. The UB is the fifth largest private university in Argentina in terms of student enrolment, with 8.3 per cent of the total of students at private universities.

Dr Avelino Porto created the Universidad de Belgrano on 11 September 1964 as a non-profit foundation in a rented building in the Belgrano neighbourhood of Buenos Aires. It featured four schools offering degrees in law, public accounts, architecture, sociology and psychology. The newly founded university had only 90 students, 28 professors and one clerk. Dr Porto was a judiciary official then and became the first Rector, a position he still holds.

The new university received only a provisional permit to begin operations, which became permanent by decree of the Executive Power in 1970, six years later. Since then, growth has been constant, with the Faculties of Law and Social Sciences, Humanities, Economics, Architecture and Urbanism added in 1964; the Faculty of Technology in 1976; Faculty of Graduate Studies in 1979; Faculties of Agrarian Sciences and Engineering in 1984; Faculty of Long Distance Studies in 1987; School of Economics and International Business in 1988; School of Software Engineering in 1989; School of Health Sciences in 1993; Faculty of Languages and Foreign Studies in 1994; and Faculty of Exact Sciences in 1995.

Colombia – Universidad de Los Andes

The Universidad de Los Andes is a non profit institution, established as a pluralist, non-religious institution, an alternative to the universities that existed at the time.

Undergraduate students reached 7,296 by the end of 1996; since it was founded, the University of Los Andes has graduated 22,000 professionals. The university now offers 26 undergraduate programmes, 15 magister[5] programmes, 21 specialisation programmes and one doctoral programme.

On 16 November 1948 a group of academics, politicians and

---

5   Colombia follows the Spanish system, with undergraduate, specialisation, magister, and doctoral degrees. The magister degrees are the approximate equivalent of Masters degrees in the USA.

influential members of Colombian society officially founded the Universidad de Los Andes, under the direction of Mr Mario Laserna. The group included 52 founders, 15 advisors and six directors. Initially, the university's programmes were architecture, economics, languages, electrical engineering, mathematics, chemistry and the School for Advanced Studies. As the institution began to grow, other programmes were offered such as civil, aeronautic, mechanical, and industrial engineering (1951). In 1955 the Schools of Engineering and Fine Arts were founded, followed by the School of Philosophy in mid-1957 and the Political Science and Anthropology Department in 1959.

Indonesia – Trisakti University

Trisakti University, one of a thousand private universities in Indonesia, was established by a decree of the government of Indonesia in November 1965. In the beginning Trisakti consisted of five faculties: Engineering, Dentistry, Medicine, Economics, and Law and Social Science. In 1995, three new faculties were added: Mineral Technology, Landscape and Environmental Technology, and Arts and Design.

The university was born out of political struggle in Indonesia, based on the site of a previous public university which had been closed by government for being 'politically incorrect'. Initially, Trisakti had 2,328 registered students, acquired from the previous public university. A memorandum of understanding was signed between Trisakti and the University of Indonesia to provide assistance to the Faculty of Medicine because of high financial costs. In addition, because many students who had been involved in subversive activities were concentrated in the Faculty of Economics, the University of Indonesia was requested to assist in the development of a 'new' model for the faculty.

In 1967, the Ministry of Higher Education put forth a proposal to convert Trisakti into a public university. However, it was decided that the university would remain as an example to other private universities. In order to fulfil its mission, the university would first remain private and second seek funding from both domestic and foreign sources for its development. By 1972, all faculties had obtained full accreditation status. In 1996–97, the total number of students was 27,481, with 1,098 full-time lecturers and 1,170 part-time lecturers.

Russia – MEPU

The International Independent University of Ecology and Political Science, Moscow (MEPU is the Russian acronym) is a non-governmental ecological university founded in 1992. It was set up in response to the perceived worsening ecological conditions, with the approval of the Ministry for Environmental Protection of the Russian Federation, the State Committee for Higher Education, the Supreme Soviet Committee on Ecology and Natural Resources and the Government of the Russian Federation.

The founders were Nikita Moiseev, an academic well known for his theory of the nuclear winter and President of the Russian Green Cross, and the rector Stanislav Stepanov, who previously worked in the Ministry of Higher Education. The aim of the university is to provide education and training to change attitudes towards the environment and develop 'ecological literacy'. The university was granted a licence to operate in 1992. In 1997, it was given accreditation by the Accrediting Board of the Ministry of

General and Higher Education, which gave it the right to award bachelor degrees. However, it does not as yet have the right to award specialist and postgraduate degrees. The university has seven faculties: Ecology, Political Science, Law, World Economy and Development, Management, Finance and State Administration, Journalism and Foreign Languages. There is also a department of Social Psychology and Ecological Tourism (which studies the effect of tourism on the environment).

MEPU started its life with a very high enrolment, which increased in 1993. At the time, there were only ten or twelve private universities and the official explanation was that of novelty together with ease of entry and unusual courses which seemed to address young people's concerns following Chernobyl, as well as the euphoria of Yeltsin's rise to power in 1992. However, in 1994 numbers plummeted. By this time *hundreds* of new universities had also received a licence.

Thailand – New International School of Thailand

The New International School of Thailand (NIST) is one of the top four international schools in Thailand, although the only one to be founded in the past 25 years. Founded in 1992, it provides English-language international education for children aged three to eighteen. Located in central Bangkok, the school serves more than 1,000 students from approximately forty different countries. NIST has established a reputation for a strong academic programme, an unusually congenial student atmosphere, and an extensive community action programme. This reputation and its central location have resulted in steady growth in enrolment. However, the school has also become known for sometimes acrimonious relations among parents. With more than forty nationalities in the school, the parents have had difficulty working together to support the school.

In March 1989, the International School of Bangkok (ISB) decided to move to a new campus far from the centre of Bangkok where the school had been established forty years earlier. Some parents objected and formed what was to become the 'UN International Education Committee', working with UNESCO backing towards the establishment of a new UN school. The Ministry granted a license in July and the New International School of Thailand opened on 13 August 1992.

Although the early years were a financial and administrative disaster, with new management in 1994 the school entered a period of more controlled growth and steady finances. This allowed the school to go ahead with the recruitment of a new headmaster, a new deputy headmaster, and additional staff to implement planned educational improvements. The most important of these advances was the establishment of the International Baccalaureate (IB) programme in the final two years of the school.

Turkey – Koç University

Koç (pronounced Koch) University is a small, young university still struggling to establish itself on a sound footing. It opened in 1993 after several years of planning and preparation. It is a non-profit institution, supported by the financial resources of the Vehbi Koç Foundation. It is an English-medium institution, with a strong foundation of liberal arts education for all students on the American model.

The Vehbi Koç Foundation is the philanthropic arm of the Koç group of companies which was built up by Vehbi Koç (1901–96). The Foundation was itself established in 1969 and channelled substantial resources into the building of elementary schools in Anatolia and student hostels in public universities, as well as the provision of scholarships for university students. A prestigious private secondary school was founded in 1988 and immediately thereafter planning began for the establishment of Turkey's second private university.

A previous group of private universities had existed in Turkey, some for many years, but these had been taken over by the state in 1971 and converted into public universities. A new law permitting the establishment of not-for-profit private universities was passed in the 1980s. Bilkent University was established soon afterwards in Ankara, and Koç University in Istanbul was to become the second of this new generation of private higher education institutions. There are now several more, but Bilkent University and Koç University are the only ones which are both financially sound and academically reputable.

Summary

The IFC global study revealed some outstanding examples of educational businesses. Of particular interest are the eleven education companies described in the first part of this chapter. They represent a previously unremarked-upon part of the private education sector, illustrating its inventiveness and innovativeness. They are all the more remarkable in that many appear to have been started on a shoe-string, under adverse circumstances, and have grown in countries where there are poorly developed credit facilities from the retail banking sector – and where education is seen as an activity scarcely worthy of credit at all.

What features have made these educational businesses successful? The next chapter examines the importance of their concern with quality control, their desire to expand in spite of financing difficulties, and the way they conduct research and development to further educational ends and to cut costs.

2 FACTORS FOR SUCCESS

We have explored some fascinating examples of private education companies in the previous chapter. The question is raised as
to what makes for a *successful* private education company or institution. Through interviews with key personnel within the institutions, students, former students and employers of students, the
study identified some key factors which make for a successful company in terms of profitability and satisfaction of the consumers. In
this chapter we highlight those factors which impact at the micro
level, on the company or institution itself. Issues concerning the
regulatory, legal and investment climates – macro factors – are
discussed in Chapter 4.

Efficiency considerations

Many of the institutions and companies examined seemed aware
of the importance of keeping costs low, by efficient use of resources such as space, technology and teacher time. For example,
NIIT, the Indian computer literacy company, goes to extreme
lengths to ensure that all resources are used productively from 7
a.m. to 10 p.m. A key part of the NIIT philosophy is in the pursuit
of teaching innovation and efficiency. Because of the economic im-
peratives – shortage of trained teachers, the expense of teachers,
and the shortage of space – NIIT from the very beginning had to be

conscious of rationing space and teacher contact time. To this end, it has used its R&D departments to develop teaching methods which reduce contact time and carefully utilise space. It has developed an educational model utilising three types of room – classroom, mind-room, and machine room – enabling a centre with only 30 computers to accommodate 1,260 students per day.

Others – for example, Educor, South Africa, Speciss College, Zimbabwe and the Brazilian chains – use classrooms for high school in the morning, then the same classrooms for further and/or higher education once high school has finished. Finally, many, including the above, operate shifts for their classes.

Innovation

We can distinguish between 'process' and 'product' innovation. The former is where businesses seek to invest in cost-reducing technologies; the latter where adjustments are made to the educational product on offer, to attract or keep customers. Both types of innovation were of importance to the educational businesses surveyed.

Research and development

It was particularly interesting to discover the great extent to which private educational companies and institutions were involved in research and development to aid innovation in both these respects.

First, this was on the level of *curriculum development*. For example:

- COC, Brazil. The curriculum is rewritten every year, and supplemented where appropriate, with new multimedia materials, for instance. Fifty personnel – including teachers and technical experts – are employed full-time in the development of these curriculum materials, to ensure that they are linked in with pedagogical and technological developments.
- Radial, Brazil. A specialised team, working in the Pedagogical Center, concentrates on curriculum development, bringing in professionals working in business and industry – especially to ensure that what is offered in the vocational courses is relevant to the state of the art of the industries concerned.
- TECSUP, Peru. In most specialities, there are annual adjustments to the curriculum, with major changes every three to five years, depending on the specialities. In information technology, however, major changes are made every year. The curriculum development process involves technical committees, with representatives from relevant industry and commerce, and annual meetings with ex-students from each specialism, who give their opinions on the relevance of the course for their work-place, and what techniques and technology are in the work-place now which need to be addressed.

Second, many of the companies engaged in R&D in all aspects of pedagogy and policy. Most notably, NIIT has two research and development departments. The first is a pure research unit, with about twenty people, many with PhDs, employed under Dr Mitra, whose brief is simply to pursue any interesting ideas in education and the cognitive sciences, without any need to look for commercial application. NIIT spends 0.7 per cent of turnover on this pure R&D (about $1 million). In part these funds are justified in terms of brand promotion – in the 1980s, NIIT was always thought of as a coaching class, and one remedy was that NIIT should be seen to generate knowledge. Just as in a university department, the productivity of the R&D is measured in terms of publications in international journals, conference attendance, etc. The second R&D department – STRIDE (Strategic Research In Development Education) – is application focused, and employs 40 researchers. It has a generic brief from senior management to look for more efficient ways of teaching, learning and course development: 'if we can teach (or a competitor) can teach this course in an hour, how can we teach it in half an hour?' Or, 'if it takes us one month to develop this course, how can we develop it in half a month?' This uses about 5 per cent of turnover.

The technological imperative

It was found to be commonplace for the education companies surveyed to be attempting to keep at the forefront of technological innovation. This imperative came for two major reasons.

First, to keep market share, and/or attract new customers – 'product' innovation. Education companies and institutions were extremely aware that if they were unable to innovate in this way, their customers would, *ceteris paribus*, take their business elsewhere. Examples include:

- TECSUP, Peru, is innovating into satellite courses, to keep and enhance its share of the company training market. The target market for the satellite courses is the mining companies outside Lima. The programme uses teachers based in Lima, in a classroom studio linked up to video and computers linked to the Internet. Students are connected to video facilities and to computers linked to the Internet, so the link-up is fully interactive.

- The COC chain of schools, Brazil, incorporates the most up-to-date technology within its schools. All classrooms are gradually being replaced by the 'classroom of the future', where all desks have their specially designed computer terminal, connected to CD-ROM and the Internet, and to the teacher's smartboard, as well as to a high brilliance projector.

- Pitágoras prides itself on being at the forefront of technological innovation. It has the following on-going projects which promote the use of telematics in the classroom:

a) Project Multimedia Class: a consultancy service which is available to all Pitágoras schools, which advises on pedagogical aspects of the introduction of multimedia, and provides educational software, training for the use of software and all equipment.

b) Project Multimedia Library: provides orientation on how to construct multimedia settings, indicating suitable educational software, etc.

c) Project Improvement of Information Technology in the School Community.

d) Project Internet: links schools to the Internet, provides consultancy about pedagogical uses of the Internet, and establishes on-line communication between school and family.

- Objetivo, Brazil, had the first school in Brazil to use interactive video for teaching, and teaching through telephone and FM radio, it was the first to introduce computers into the classroom, and the first to use CD-ROM multimedia for classroom instruction. The Tarefa Net (Homework Net) allows students to do homework exercises in an interactive form on the Internet. The student can access solutions to problems in a step-by-step manner, and have hypertext links to related problems and ideas. Objetivo also makes use of the 'Disque-professor', a service whereby any student who has difficulties solving problems in the published curriculum materials, or tests, can telephone the central computing office, code in the relevant number, and receive a commentary on questions, 24 hours a day.
- DPS, India, is presently in talks with ISRO (the Indian Space Research Organisation) for the leasing of satellite time and the creation of VSAT links, which will lead to satellite- and Internet-based distance education programmes. It is anticipated that this will be funded through donations, grants and soft loans from the corporate sector, as well as through subscriptions from the member schools.

Second, some companies and institutions are aware that through technological innovation they are able to cut costs – 'process' innovation. For example:

- TECSUP, Peru, is developing a 'virtual university', which will deliver courses to students across its campuses, enabling the same teacher and materials to be used, hence considerably reducing costs over the long term; it also aims to develop the lucrative distance learning for corporations outside of the capital city.

- CODECS, Romania, is acquiring a satellite tele-conference system, in order to transfer its British MBA programme from the UK at considerably lower costs. Tutors will still be from the UK, but the tele-conference system will eliminate the significant travel costs currently incurred bringing them to Romania.

Brand name

It challenged some of our preconceptions about education to discover the importance of brand name, and the promotion thereof in some of the educational companies. As noted above, the desire to inform consumers through the brand name is of great significance in countering one of the foremost objections to private education, that consumers will suffer from an intractable information problem. For example, any visitor to South Africa cannot fail to be struck by the ubiquity of advertisements for courses offered by Damelin and other Educor subsidiaries – covering high school, university courses and vocational and professional courses; a visitor to Brazil will soon come across billboard advertising for Objetivo/UNIP, COC or Pitágoras – for the full range from kindergarten to university; in India, the brand name of NIIT is everywhere – on television, radio and in print – advertising computer courses for undergraduates, professional training and, increasingly, computer literacy courses in schools and at home.

Brand name was significant in this way for about half of the case studies surveyed, viz. Objetivo/UNIP, COC, Pitágoras, Radial, Educor, Speciss College, TECSUP, NIIT and CODECS.

Perhaps not surprisingly, for the stand-alone schools and universities such as Los Andes, Koç, Belgrano, Trisakti and NIST it was far less significant. What factors contribute to making brand promotion so important? A few factors worth noting in this regard are as follows:

- Companies concerned with brand promotion could be for-profit or not-for-profit
- Brand promotion covered the whole range of education reviewed – from kindergarten, primary and high school, to university, as well as vocational and professional courses
- Not all concerned with brand promotion are *large* chains – TECSUP has only two campuses, and Speciss College, Zimbabwe, four. Furthermore, not all large chains need brand promotion – Delhi Public Schools (DPS) with 42 schools does very little to promote itself, relying on its long established reputation. (The combination of having been in the market since 1947, and in a market with considerable excess demand, is perhaps not replicable elsewhere.)

For those companies which are concerned to promote their brand names the following general comments can be made:

- Advertising can amount to about 10 per cent of turnover
- Companies have full-time marketing staff and management to develop and strengthen brand name
- A variety of methods and promotions is used to strengthen brand name
- Companies can successfully pursue a 'dual-brand' strategy
- Independent market research shows the brand-name

promotion to have been successful for many companies, although some company-based research also shows that the majority of clients actually heard about the courses through word-of-mouth recommendation, rather than advertising.

Some examples illustrate these themes.

Educor, South Africa

Educor does direct selling in private and government schools. Other brand-promoting events include careers evenings and road-shows and softball and volleyball tournaments.

Speciss College, Zimbabwe

The most dramatic *range* of activities to promote brand name was found in Speciss College, Zimbabwe. These include: the sponsoring of a basketball team and two national athletes; careers days at all state and private high schools; running of film premiers under the Speciss banner; an elaborate graduation each year with a high media profile; giving away courses as prizes in charity raffles; and high profile Mr Speciss Personality and Miss Speciss contests.

It seems clear that this promotion of the brand name has succeeded. Recent market research shows Speciss to be the leader when respondents were asked, unprompted, for their knowledge of tertiary education institutions. It was the highest rated for blacks and Asians/mixed race, although it came third for whites. Combined ratings for spontaneous and prompted awareness put Speciss in third place, after the University of Zimbabwe and the Polytechnic.

NIIT, India

NIIT pursues aggressive newspaper advertising, but also successfully ran its own radio show, now replaced by an equally successful television show 'Boot It'. This is in a commercial slot, financed by selling advertising space at the beginning, middle and end of the programme, which aims to introduce people to the world of computing – and also acts as a marketing conduit to further NIIT courses. It is advertised as a free computer literacy programme for the masses, and is a 24-episode series broadcast on metro and national channels. It is also broadcast in Pakistan and Mauritius. This TV show was launched in July 1997, although it had been ready for broadcasting for the previous eighteen months, but had been held up by government regulation.

Again, NIIT's brand-building seems to be highly successful. Recent Gallup research shows that, just as people use 'making a Xerox' as synonymous with 'making a photocopy', so 'doing an NIIT' is synonymous with 'studying a computer course'. Some employers are now advertising that they are seeking someone 'with an Indian University Master's degree, or GNIIT'.

COC, Brazil

COC has its own publicity department – PubliCOC – which plans and implements its media strategies, develops advertisements and supports other developments of its brand name. Marketing techniques include advertising in newspapers, magazines, on radio and television. It also sponsors a nationally renowned basketball team – PoltiCOC – which takes part in the highest level competitions in Brazil. Also having its own TV and radio stations, used for general broadcasting (not just educational material), helps promote its brand name all year round.

Delhi Public Schools, India

By virtue of its high reputation and excess demand for its schooling, DPS has had no need for any active marketing effort, other than to announce the dates when it opens admissions at its respective schools. Even as far as new school ventures are concerned the management has no need to go out and canvass prospective promoters for joint ventures – in fact, the members of the Working Committee are besieged with applications for joint venture schools. Although there are huge numbers of other, competing, private schools, demand is such that their success seems to have had absolutely no impact on the operations of the DPS. Interestingly, in the event that a family is transferred from one location to another part of the country, it is an understood condition that if a DPS family school exists in the new location the children will be given preference and generally granted automatic admission into the other DPS branch. This clearly helps strengthen brand, without advertising.

Pitágoras, Brazil

Pitágoras does use normal marketing routes, such as media advertising. However, a key aspect of the promotion of its brand name comes from its social responsibility programme: the 'Projeto Pitágoras-JB' involves the distribution of a free newspaper, in partnership with the *Jornal do Brasil*, eventually aiming to reach every school in Brazil each week. Pitágoras's name appears on every page, although in an unobtrusive way.

Certification

A successful educational institution must offer respected and recognised qualifications. Five options emerged from the case studies. First, the institution or company can offer its own certification:

- Educor subsidiaries, South Africa, offer their own certification, including Damelin Certificates and Diplomas and Allenby Prestige Diplomas
- At Speciss College, Zimbabwe, the cheapest *and* the most expensive courses offered lead solely to Speciss College Certificates
- NIIT, India, offer its own certificates, leading to the GNIIT
- Objetivo/UNIP offers its own certification at both the school and university level
- Universidad de Los Andes, Colombia, offers its own degrees, as does MEPU, Russia.

Second, the institution or company can offer qualifications accredited by outside, recognised institutions:

- Educor subsidiaries offer courses leading to British and UNISA degrees, and British and South African professional institute diplomas
- Speciss offers courses leading to British, South African and Zimbabwean professional institute qualifications
- NIST, Thailand, offers the International Baccalaureate and IGCSE (Cambridge, UK), as well as the NIST diploma
- CODECS offers British Open University degrees
- TECSUP offers MBA courses from a Spanish university.

Third, the institution or company can offer a combination of these – own certificates endorsed by professional bodies, or incorporating outside certificates:

- Many of the one-year courses offered by Damelin lead to Damelin Diplomas endorsed by professional bodies
- Speciss' Executive Secretarial Course leads to Pitman (UK) examinations *and* the Speciss Certificate.

Fourth, the company or institution can offer qualifications jointly with other institutions:

- Universidad Belgrano, Argentina, as well as offering its own degrees, grants joint degrees with French, American and Spanish universities.

Fifth, the company or institution can offer certification which is worth credits in other institutions:

- NIIT, India has negotiated that one of its courses is worth 27 credits towards an MBA in American universities, negotiated with the American Council on Education
- Universidad Belgrano, Argentina has mutual credit recognition agreements with foreign universities, including 156 US universities.

The first option, own certification, seemed to be possible only under three conditions:

- where a strong brand name already exists

- where there is the backing of a strong brand name (for example, Allenby backed by Midrand Campus, Educor); or
- where the university (only) has been granted the right to award degrees by the government's accrediting authority.

The other four options are possible in any institution, and have been used explicitly, we were told, by companies wishing to build up the credibility of their brand names. Interestingly, once their credibility has been established, this does not mean that the method is abandoned. For example, Damelin, South Africa, may have needed the endorsement of the professional associations to help establish credibility; now that it is well known, it maintains the endorsement.

Integration and expansion

Integration has been a preoccupation of many of the companies in our case studies. Many of the successful companies studied have expanded their operations through 'horizontal' integration, taking over other schools or companies; others have integrated 'laterally', diversifying into other levels of educational delivery, or related trades such as recruitment; a few firms have integrated 'vertically', by taking over the educational publishing process, including multimedia development.

Horizontal integration: taking over other schools

Three of the four Brazilian chains studied (Objetivo/UNIP, COC and Pitágoras) began life as pre-university cramming classes, and then developed in all three cases by expanding downwards into high school, elementary school and finally kindergarten. Sometimes this was accomplished by taking over existing schools, although other times by opening new schools. The fourth chain, Radial, began as an evening technical college, but took over an existing high school and elementary school, before opening other new schools from scratch.

In southern Africa, Educor, South Africa and Speciss College, Zimbabwe, both started as cramming colleges too, and have since taken over other colleges.

Vertical integration: moving into new levels of education

Many of the companies studied have moved into new levels of education. Some examples are:

- Objetivo/UNIP, Brazil, opened a university chain, while COC, Brazil is seeking to do the same
- Educor, South Africa and Speciss, Zimbabwe, have moved into all areas from high school, through vocational and technical education, to university
- NIIT, India, has moved from computer training to managing 'edutainment' opportunities for children and parents in schools and neighbourhood centres.

Lateral integration: synergy between education and recruitment

Many education companies have found 'synergy' between education and recruitment, both as a marketing tool and as a way of enhancing the educational experience offered.

In NIIT, India, each centre has an RIIC (Regional Industry Collaboration Cell), whose task is to keep continually in touch with information technology CEOs and recruitment personnel, both in order to get a feel for what is needed in the market, and to help place students. It keeps a detailed database of all students, and matches individuals to the recruitment needs of particular companies.

TECSUP, Peru, has a small but specialised department which keeps in constant contact with a huge number of companies, and with students placed within those companies.

Radial, Brazil, also has extensive contacts with companies and can help in the placement of graduates in work – it has a concordat with more than 200 companies. Moreover, many of the teachers, including at high school, are part-time, working in companies, and it runs internships for its teachers to have a term in business or industry, both in part to further promote these contacts.

The connection between recruitment and education has been realised by education companies buying recruitment agencies (Educor, South Africa), or by recruitment agencies buying education companies (ADvTECH – not one of the case studies – in South Africa).

Lateral and vertical integration: television and radio

Three of the Brazilian chains studied – COC, Pitágoras and Objetivo/UNIP – have moved into radio and television, and other media, initially as a way of extending their control over educational media (vertical integration), but also as a way of diversifying their portfolio. The most dramatic example is COC, and its '*Sistema COC de Educação e Comunicação*'. COC prides itself on being a combined system of education and communication. To this end it has a movie theatre, to supplement the cultural activities of its students, and TV and radio stations. COC Cinema is based in Ribeirão Preto, and provides film viewings for its students (and employees) free of charge, 'to reinforce the classroom experience'. These include foreign and art movies which otherwise would be hard for students to find. Its place in the city centre also ensures the continued promotion of the COC brand name. COC also has two TV stations, one a commercial television station, which broadcasts programmes to a region of over five million people, the second is totally dedicated to education. It works jointly with Fundacão Roquete Pinto (an educational foundation), to broadcast programmes made by TV Educativa do Rio de Janeiro (one of the two educational TV stations in Brazil).

Vertical integration: publishing and multimedia development

Many companies have moved into educational publishing and multimedia development as a way of having control over the educational process:

- COC, Brazil, runs its own publishing house, Editora COC, which publishes educational books, workbooks, supporting charts and CD-ROMs
- Objetivo has a similar publishing house and multimedia development centre
- CODECS, Romania, has a publishing house, translating and printing business books in Romania, in co-operation with

foreign publishers such as Amacom, Gower, Kogan Page, Crisp, Pitman
- NIIT has the largest educational software development centre anywhere in the world, developing multimedia CD-ROM and Internet course materials
- Educor (Damelin), South Africa and Speciss College, Zimbabwe publish study guides, both for their own students and for others
- MEPU, Russia, has a small publishing department, with ten full-time and three or four part-time staff. It publishes books for courses in law, management, foreign languages and journalism.

Other expansion

It is also noteworthy the way in which many educational companies have expanded throughout their respective countries, with many expanding internationally. Notable international expansion includes:

- NIIT has more than 400 centres around India, and operates in eighteen countries worldwide, including Indonesia, Singapore, China, Zimbabwe, Botswana and the USA
- Educor has more than 40 centres and franchises around South Africa, and has expanded into Namibia, Botswana, Malawi and Lesotho, with expansion into Zimbabwe and Mauritius imminent.

Raising capital

How have the education companies financed their expansion? Surprisingly, most of the companies surveyed had never borrowed, but had started as shoestring operations, and had financed all their expansion through internal equity investment. Examples of companies following this route were the Brazilian chains of COC, Objetivo/UNIP, Pitágoras and Radial, and CODECS in Romania. In other cases we found companies which had also started on a shoestring, which had financed all their initial expansion through internal investment, but which later were able to finance expansion through rights issues. Examples here were Educor and ADvTECH in South Africa, and NIIT in India.

However, the fact that so few of the companies or institutions surveyed had gone the loan route should be interpreted with some caution because it was almost always found in addition that:

- Loans were avoided because internal interest rates were too high (with annual figures of 30–80 per cent cited)
- Many institutions felt that they would be unattractive to banks, at least in the early stages, because they did not have enough collateral for loans
- It was felt that banks were in any case unfamiliar with education as a business that needed investment
- There were poorly developed capital markets in many of the countries surveyed.

Hence, just because many of the companies have not used debt financing in the past does not mean that similar companies would not be inclined to use it now, if the first three of these caveats could be overcome. Moreover, several of the successful company directors interviewed also agreed that they would not be averse to seeking debt financing now if the conditions were acceptable.[6]

Franchising

For many education companies surveyed, franchising was a very important strategy for expansion. In vocational education NIIT franchised computer centres, as did Educor (Damelin); in school education, all the Brazilian chains had franchises – sometimes as many as 450 (Objetivo). Interestingly, Objetivo only franchised at the school, not university, level, feeling that quality control would be too tricky at the latter level. However, MEPU, the ecological university in Russia, has a franchise agreement, to allow other universities to provide their ecology course (only) to the specification

---

6   Support for the potential of the private education sector to respond to more favourable capital markets can be seen from the experience of education companies in the United States (see, for example, Education Securities Inc., *Newsletter*, Nos. 4–8, 1997). In the US there is an active debt market for private education institutions and companies, both at the university and school level, although debt to capitalisation ratios are generally fairly low (in the region of 10–35 per cent). Many of the larger non-profit US education companies, at both the secondary and university level, use debt issuance of bonds. For instance, higher education institutions in the US issued $9.77 billion of bonds in 1996. It is notable that 45 private K-12 schools have received investment grade ratings from either Moody's or Standard and Poor, while 60 per cent of private K-12 schools in one survey had debt on their balance sheet. A range of factors is used by the rating agencies in evaluating the credit of private schools, including marketing issues, diversity of their revenue sources, debt service, profitability, current facilities and management structure. It should be noted that, unlike most of the companies examined in the current report, the non-profit US companies frequently have significant endowments, and these are considered by lenders in their appraisal of creditworthiness. One source suggests that, for a K-12 school, maximum debt service should be less than 10 per cent of operations.

of MEPU. Thus just one course, not the whole university concept, is franchised.

Two distinct ways of franchising were discovered:

- The franchisee pays a percentage of income to the mother company in return for use of the brand name, training and use of materials. This was found in Educor and ADvTECH in South Africa, MEPU in Russia, NIIT and ApTECH in India, and FutureKids worldwide.
- The franchise buys the curriculum materials from the mother company (or its publishing arm). Along with the materials comes the package of quality control mechanisms that make the school entitled to use the brand name. This was the case in the Brazilian chains (COC, Objetivo and Pitágoras).

Income received from franchises as a percentage of total income varied considerably. NIIT received 20 per cent of its total income in 1996 from franchise royalties, whereas Educor received only 3 per cent.

Quality control

If education companies are expanding, and especially if they are doing this through franchising, then quality control becomes of key concern to these companies, if the strength of their brand is to be sustained. How do the various head offices keep control over their disparate sites? Some examples illustrate the degree to which quality control – and hence the maintaining of the esteem of the brand name – are of paramount importance to the education companies surveyed:

NIIT

NIIT, India, exercises tight control over its 400 franchises and 30 branches. Since January 1995, it has implemented CCQMS (Crosby's Complete Quality Management System). Each member of staff undergoes the same initial and in-service training at head office or a regional centre, and all management must also have been NIIT teachers. Each course tutor is given a batch file, which describes in meticulous detail all the courses to be taught, the sub-units, the material to be covered, and the time to be taken on each section – this even prescribes how long must be taken over each overhead transparency! To complement this, each tutor follows a standardised quality control procedure, monitored initially within the branch, then by quality control visits from central or regional management. This procedure uses the following indicators:

- Aggregated mean student marks, as taken on NIIT standardised tests twice a semester (marked by someone other than the faculty). If students are doing badly on these objective tests, this is seen to reflect badly on the faculty member.
- Student feedback questionnaire, completed three times a semester, on which they rate the faculty, the NIIT and their own learning. Importantly, one of the questions asks for the student's *own grasp* of the knowledge. If the student gives a low assessment here, this reflects badly on *the individual faculty member*.
- Student upgrades. If students are initially only registered for one semester (as about 50 per cent are), then if they reregister for another course, this is taken as a point in the faculty member's favour.

- Student defaulters. If students default on payment or drop out of a course, this is taken as a negative indicator of the faculty member.

Educor (Damelin), South Africa

All 43 branches and franchises of Damelin are subject to identical quality control procedures. They run exactly the same courses, with teachers following identical course materials, using centrally agreed assignments and assessments, in classrooms laid out to identical minimum specifications, and so on. There are detailed specifications about who can be employed, and all lecturers are evaluated three times a year, using a standardised Lecturer Evaluation Questionnaire, filled out by students. To oversee all these quality control procedures, there is a specialised department, the National Support Office, headed by the National Director of Studies, and a team of full-time administrators.

Objetivo, Brazil

A key aspect of Objetivo's quality control is based on the course materials. It is prescribed that these are used in exactly the same way throughout the country. All teachers have to finish the same syllabus by the end of each month. If they do not cover all the lessons, then they have to give extra lessons during the month until they do. (Teachers do not see this as restricting their professional autonomy – they see themselves as presenters of material, rather than adjudicators of what that material should be: 'it is part of what it means to be a teacher, to be a performer').

Pitágoras, Brazil

All Pitágoras schools have to follow common quality control procedures, involving their version of Total Quality Management (TQM) involving standardised tests and surveys of parents. Pitágoras's TQM workshops have been attended by over 4,000 professionals from all over Brazil, and, with the help of the Juran Institute, USA, have been exported to the USA. The Total Quality Office has now become a separate wholly-owned group company, the *Pitágoras TEC*; it is involved in preparation of consultants for the implementation of TQM in education, benchmarking in schools, and problem solving for continuous improvement. Broadly speaking, the quality management programme is based on the careful articulation of a school's vision and mission, in terms of five objectives:

1. high performance for all, and improvement of institutions
2. enhanced competence of the teaching workforce – to enable high student performance
3. social responsibility programme
4. relations of partnership – in particular between parents and schools
5. TQM.

Objectives 2–5 are to enable objective 1 to be achieved.

These are then set out in more detail in the General Improvement Plan, in terms of *goals* and *measures and results*, which demonstrate whether the outcomes have been achieved.

For example, the first objective of 'raising standards' is spelled out in terms of 'specific competencies'; goals such as 'each student must be able to read and understand different kinds of materials, and apply them at the level of their own study level; each student must write, read, listen and use information technology to communicate,' etc. The measures and results are specified in terms of passing external examinations, Vestibular examinations, and internal Pitágoras evaluations.

Similarly, the second objective of 'improving the competence of the workforce' is spelled out in terms of goals such as 'the professionals will be involved in making decisions which most affect them'; 'the opportunities for personal and professional development must reflect the strategic directions of Pitágoras group'; 'the evaluation tools of the professionals must provide incentives for continual improvement'. The appropriate measures and results include such things as 'percentage of professionals engaged in quality improvement programme'; 'introduction of a suggestions programme'; 'perception of professionals in own involvement in making decisions'; 'number of opportunities in education and training which reflect the strategic directions of Pitágoras'.

The third objective of social responsibility is specified in terms of goals such as students participating in social projects, and leaders participating and taking the initiative. Measures and results include the number of projects and evaluation of the effectiveness of these projects, including the perceptions of the educative community.

The fourth objective of improving relationships is specified in terms of goals such as 'each school will involve in an active way the families in order to reach the highest level of skills of the students'. The measures and results include the number of initiatives which involve families, together with evaluation of their effectiveness, including the perceptions of all those involved.

Finally, the TQM objective has goals such as that 'information systems will be created to support the aims of the group and the improvement process'. The measures and results include the number of schools and departments which use the integrated management system, and which have information systems in place.

Donations and endowments

A key question initially posed for the research was whether there are schools and universities which could make a surplus without endowments and donations, for only in such cases would it be considered that private education could be genuinely self-sufficient and sustainable. Of the cases examined, several were set up using donations, or established with endowments, including the universities of Koç (Turkey), Trisakti (Indonesia) and MEPU (Russia); at school level, NIST (Thailand), and the technical vocational establishment of TECSUP (Peru). However, the majority were not, but these were able to survive and, indeed, prosper, without any donations or endowments.

Clearly, as not enough institutions in the same country were studied, we were not able to draw definite conclusions about differences between these types of institutions. Nevertheless, it is perhaps worth making a few comments based on the admittedly sparse evidence gained, given the political importance attached in many countries to the issue of whether educational institutions could be allowed to be for-profit.

First, sometimes donations particularly from overseas donors come with strings attached. This can lead to a distortion of what is offered in the educational institution. For example, one of the case studies revealed overseas donors requiring of the institution:

- fees that were artificially low – that is, lower than could easily be afforded by the great majority of students
- student numbers that were artificially low – that is, lower than could be satisfactorily (although not luxuriously) accommodated in the facilities
- scholarships to the poor that did not have to be repaid, rather than offering loans which could eventually add to the institution's income, and to the students' sense of responsibility.

Each of these, it seemed, led to unnecessary inefficiencies, and, in turn, an increased reliance on the need for external donations.

Second, it did not seem that such foundations were necessarily more concerned for the disadvantaged than those operating on a for-profit basis.

Third, it did not seem to be the case, as might be expected, that those foundations receiving donations and with endowments were able to offer less expensive or higher quality courses than those which did not have donations or endowments.

These three factors suggest that there may be disadvantages to companies and institutions of seeking donations and/or endowments.

For-profit versus not-for-profit

A related issue concerns whether companies are for-profit, or not-for-profit. As can be seen from Table 2 on pp. 36–7, roughly 50 per cent of the companies or institutions surveyed were for-profit, and 50 per cent not-for-profit. What difference does this make to educational institutions and companies? The hypothesis that

emerges from our study – in parallel with that concerning donations and endowments – would be that there is not much difference between these types of companies in terms of 'profitability'
(or creating a surplus), educational efficacy and equity. For example, it might be thought by some that not-for-profit companies
would be more inclined to invest their surpluses in expansion and
improvements, and the for-profit companies more inclined to pay
dividends, but this did not seem to be borne out by the evidence
here. The for-profit companies such as NIIT, COC and Educor
seem to be among the biggest investors in expansion and quality
improvement.

Why do companies and institutions follow the 'not-for-profit'
route in education? There would seem to be four reasons.

- The 'moral' reason: for-profit education is seen as an
  oxymoron, or is, at least, less desirable than not-for-profit
- For-profit education is illegal
- Education companies or institutions wish to have the benefits
  of being not-for-profit foundations, including not paying
  taxes, and being able to receive donations which companies
  can set against taxation
- Big companies wish to use their funds in a philanthropic way
  and avoid taxes, so set up not-for-profit educational
  institutions.

In many of the countries surveyed, the second reason was to
the fore: for-profit education is illegal. This is true, for example,
for Indonesia, Peru (when TECSUP was set up, although this has
now been relaxed), Romania, Russia and Argentina. In India, this
restriction has been incorporated into its constitution. India's

relevant constitutional guideline is clear on this issue:

> The promoting body cannot distribute its surplus, if any, at
> the end of a year, but must plough it back into Reserves or
> further Capital Expenditure. Surpluses can, however, be
> used to service loans or pay lease money.

The third reason probably lay behind TECSUP's establishment as a not-for-profit foundation, so that it could receive donations from other companies. Koç University, Turkey, was set up as a foundation in large part for the fourth reason.

Many analysts question whether non-profit institutions can achieve the level of benefits of full market competition. Several associated inefficiencies have been recognised by economists for some time. Non-profit decision-makers choose quantity–quality mixes of output, for instance, that are optimal for them but not necessarily for society. Second there is a strong probability of expropriation of the non-profit's surpluses by its agents (West, 1989). This can be done for instance via salary increases and perks on the job.

Apparently there are some ways to 'get around' the strict regulations against educational for-profit institutions. Thus NIIT has been able to escape the restriction in India because it is registered under the Companies Act, rather than as an educational institution. In Romania, while the Education Law stipulates that education must be organised and function on non-profit principles, the same law allows institutions, *including commercial companies*, to deliver professional training programmes of adults through distance learning. It is through this channel that CODECS has been able to operate.

Leased versus owned property

Another of the major issues for the IFC, although perhaps of less importance to a more general reader, concerned the level of owned facilities appropriate to different educational opportunities. This study found that it did not seem to be a particularly relevant criterion for success in private education, with successful education companies either leasing or owning property, or both. One of the suggestions was that leased property may be hard to adapt for educational uses. However, we have found educational companies leasing unsuitable buildings and drastically renovating them – even though leases have been short. Or we found educational companies leasing purpose-built educational buildings. In many countries, there are inflexible planning regulations which often mean that any building involves considerable bribes. In India this situation is exacerbated by extremely high capital gains tax, which means that buying and selling of property may require money laundering. NIIT aims to steer clear of these problems by never owning property, and so takes out leases. However, leasing buildings does not stop it extensively modifying them to suit its requirements. This is so even though may of the buildings are on leases of only three years (described as 'long leases'!).

Management of risk of non-payment of tuition fees

This is a key area which will make for the success or otherwise of a private educational institution or company, particularly one which is funded almost entirely by fees – as in the majority of the case studies considered. Annual bad debt runs at about 5 to 6 per cent of turnover in many of the successful companies observed. Methods of countering the problem of bad debt include the following:

- 'cash' only colleges
- internal and external debt control – including rescheduling terms of payment, employing internal debt control offices and contracting external debt collectors
- smart card systems
- providing employment for debtors
- introducing student loan systems.

We outline methods for the first four of these, and explore the fifth further in the following chapter.

Cash colleges

In southern Africa, 'cash' colleges, that is, working on cash-only terms, are a popular way of avoiding the risk of non-payment. Speciss College operates two 'cash' colleges, Magaba and what used to be Lobengula, now part of Bulawayo campus. Similarly, some of the Damelin courses (that is, not whole campuses) are specifically 'cash only'. Students are only allowed in if they have paid (usually) the monthly instalment of their fees in advance. This seems to work in practice, leading to a drop-out rate as high as 20 per cent; however, students can miss a month, then come back to class when their financial position improves. (There is a monthly intake onto courses, so students can learn more or less at their own pace.)

Internal and external debt control

Many institutions offer (usually) monthly terms of payment for courses. At Educor, the chief counter to the bad debt problem is to ensure that, at registration, all students sign a contract to pay all the tuition fees even if they withdraw from the course. Defaulters are then referred to the Credit Control Department. Similar procedures were found in a variety of places, including Speciss College and NIIT.

Smart cards

More advanced methods of avoiding bad debt include the issue of smart cards, which contain all relevant registration information. At the University of Belgrano, Argentina, each student must register for each class using this card. If a student is in arrears and has not requested any special payment terms, he/she is not recorded as present in the class. As students are required to attend 80 per cent of their classes in order to be able to sit examinations, the incentive for payment or rearranging terms is very strong.

A smart card scheme is also used at Midrand Campus, part of Educor, South Africa. Here students have to use their card in order to enter and leave campus. Initially if they fall behind with their payments, their card will not let them *leave* campus. Hence, they will be forced to go to administration, and reschedule payment of fees before being permitted to exit. After a period of time in which options are explored, the smart card will then refuse entry to the student too. The theory behind this is that the campus does not want to exclude students unless all payment options have been exhausted.

However, not all places that use smart cards also use them to deter bad debts. In the Brazilian chains of Objetivo/UNIP and COC, smart cards are not programmed in this way.

Providing employment

When students or their parents are unable to pay instalments on fees at Koç University, Turkey (having already paid their first down-payment), then students will be offered part-time employment within the university to help them to earn the funds required, when this is possible to find. This could include cleaning, serving or tutoring roles.

Summary

This chapter has highlighted some of the factors at the micro level which have led to the success of the educational businesses surveyed. The IFC study was concerned with *success* defined in terms of the companies' profitability – and from this we can infer that all the businesses described here were successful in attracting and satisfying customers. Given the case study methodology employed, we were not able to judge which of the factors were most significant for success. However, in the views of key personnel within the companies, as well as students, former students and employers of students, we have seen that factors involving efficiency and innovation – particularly in terms of technology to cut costs and enhance the educational experiences on offer – were of key importance. Research and development to these ends were also of significance, as was the promoting of the brand name and using recognised certification. Many of the companies surveyed were keen to expand and integrate their activities; successful expansion often involved franchising, and in all cases strict quality control procedures were a key part of making for success.

These factors may satisfy investors and international organisations such as the IFC and the World Bank that such investment is viable. However, some readers may be apprehensive about seeking to enhance the role of the private sector in any development strategy, because of the paramount objection of the perceived inequity of private education. Tackling this objection is the subject of the next chapter.

3   EQUITY ISSUES

A common perception of private education in developing countries is that it caters mainly for the élite, and hence that its promotion will only increase inequity. The argument of this chapter is that this may not be the case, for five reasons:

- Because the IFC study reveals a vast range of private education opportunities, not just catering for the élite or even the middle classes
- Because public education itself is not generally free, and when hidden costs of schooling are introduced, the differences between costs of private and public education are narrowed considerably
- Public funding of education can also be inequitable
- Because of impact on gender equity
- Educational businesses can help promote equity through cross- subsidisation, social responsibility programmes and involvement with the public sector, and, perhaps most significantly, through student loan programmes.

The first four of these issues are grouped under the heading 'macro issues', while the fifth is discussed under the heading 'company-level issues'.

Macro issues

Range of private education opportunities

A common prejudice against private education is that it only serves the élite. The IFC study shows this not to be the case. There are numerous examples of institutions which charge relatively modest fees, making them accessible to a broad range of socio-economic groups. In general, we can point to the existence of *three* types of private *schools*. First, there are schools which cater for very low income groups in rural or urban areas, charging very low fees, and offering education of variable quality – usually with high student/teacher ratios (up to 90 students per teacher), offering a basic education with no frills. They can be run by charities or religious groups, or be run by proprietors. In India, for example, these schools charge fees ranging from Rs. 50 to Rs. 150 per month, and are usually sponsored by local philanthropists or by religious or minority charitable organisations. In South Africa, there are still many 'street' schools, operating in rural and urban areas, catering for similar groups.

Second, there are schools that are patronised by the middle classes, including religious not-for-profit and for-profit. The Brazilian chains of schools largely fit into this category, while the Delhi Public School chain caters for similar children in India. It must be noted, however, that sometimes extended families can pool income to enable one or more children from the family to attend such schools.[1]

---

1   In many countries surveyed – for example, South Africa, India and Brazil – it was initially a puzzle as to how many of the students could afford to attend educational institutions whose fees would seem prohibitive given reported family income. Further probing made it apparent that it may be misleading to look at *individual* family incomes alone. The puzzle was resolved when it was discovered how extended families pooled income and resources to support one or more

Third, there are the élite private schools, found in all countries, with fees out of the reach of all except a small minority – although many of these schools do offer scholarships to students whose parents are too poor, or who fall on hard times while the student is at the school.

In terms of *vocational* tertiary education, opportunities were found which generally catered for lower and middle socio-economic groups, and it is clear that many low-income families make large sacrifices to enable their children to attend secretarial courses and other job-related training courses that could provide rapid returns – as well as pooling income as noted above.

Finally, in terms of *academic* tertiary education, private universities generally catered for the middle and upper income groups. Interestingly, there were some examples of the non-élite private universities being used more by lower income groups than the prestigious public universities – for example, in Brazil (Objetivo/UNIP), Romania and Russia.

Costs of public education relative to private education

Public education in developing countries does not usually come free of costs to families, and, in particular, to poor families. This is true first in terms of *direct* costs – for in many countries, public schools either charge school fees (for example, South Africa), or charge registration and examination fees (for example, Indonesia),

---

particularly talented, ambitious and industrious children within the family. This practice was found at both compulsory schooling and tertiary-level (academic and vocational) education. Hence, promising students from some of the poorest families are able to attend institutions even though the fees would seem to put them out of reach, considering the low level of the *individual's* family income.

or 'encourage' parents to contribute additional funds, which effectively make up *de facto* fees (for example, Argentina, Indonesia, and Turkey). There are also *indirect* costs of schooling, such as transportation, writing materials and school uniform.

When these indirect costs are taken into account, the gap between annual household expenditure for a public and private school student narrows considerably. Where figures are available, the picture emerges of:

- significant costs of public education for poor families
- a large gap between the costs associated with public and private education at the primary school level
- a narrowing of the gap at secondary levels of schooling.

The examples of India and Indonesia are given to illustrate these points.

In India, average household expenditure (including indirect costs of public schooling, and full direct costs of private schooling) on each student in the poorest 20 per cent of households was about Rs. 60 per year for students in public schools, but Rs. 113 per year, or 90 per cent more, for a student in a private school. (Annual income for these families was Rs. 8,274; all figures for 1991.) At the secondary level, however, the average household expenditure was Rs. 230 per year in the state sector, compared to Rs. 291, or only 26 per cent more, in the private sector.

For the next poorest 20 per cent of households (annual income Rs. 12,528), household expenditure per student in primary school was roughly twice as much in a private than in a public school (Rs. 139 compared with Rs. 71), but only one fifth more for private secondary school students (Rs. 286, compared with Rs. 241). These margins were roughly comparable throughout the socio-economic levels, except for the top 20 per cent of the population, where household expenditure on primary school children was three and a half times as much for families with students in private schools.

In Indonesia, compulsory school fees for primary and junior secondary schools were abolished in 1973 and 1994–95 respectively. However, almost all schools receive contributions from their parents' association. Some of these contributions are 'one-off' entrance fees, some are monthly fees and some are 'special assessments' for particular purposes. Such fees are not officially compulsory, but are in fact expected in most situations. In *primary education*, the average annual expenditure by Indonesian families per student for *public* education is Rp 52,000, 25 per cent of which is paid directly to the school for registration and examination fees, and the remainder is made up by indirect costs. The average total cost to families for *private* education, however, is Rp 122,000 per year, covering direct fees and indirect costs. Thus private primary education costs households roughly two and one-third times as much as public primary education.

At *junior secondary education*, however, the gap begins to narrow, with average annual expenditure by Indonesian families per student in *public* school being Rp 144,000 (of which a third is paid directly to the school), whereas the cost of *private* education averages Rp 216,000 per student per year, or only 50 per cent more. At *senior secondary education*, average costs are Rp 229,000 for *public (general)* and Rp 262,000 for *public (vocational)* schools, with 35–40 per cent of this in direct costs to the school. For *private (general)* and *private (vocational)*, annual household costs are Rp 314,000 and Rp 338,000 respectively, or only 30 per cent more. Interestingly, at the Islamic schools in Indonesia, average annual household expenditure per student for private and public schools is roughly comparable.

Finally, we note that in Argentina, as a result of the continuing crisis in public education, parents of public school students organised into 'cooperadora' to support their schools with voluntary contributions. This has become so embedded in the system that it has become a *de facto* quota paid by all students. The 1994 Census shows that 90 per cent of public schools had such a mechanism of financing. This means that parents are paying for public education and in some cases those payments are not much different from the quotas charged by private schools, even though the latter may give services (such as language and computer learning) which the public sector does not provide. A similar situation pertains in Turkey.

Inequity in public education funding

Next we consider how total public spending in education in low-income countries typically favours the affluent, and indeed can often be a subsidy from the less well-off to the higher income groups. Considerable research evidence supports this claim, from developed as well as developing countries (see, for example, Le Grand, 1987; Barr, 1993; World Bank, 1994; Bray, 1996; Hanushek, 1995; West, 1997; Ziderman and Douglas, 1995). This situation applies because fewer low-income children attend secondary and higher education institutions. In this context, the benefits of increasing the number of students in private education as a strategy for development are twofold. For it would: (a) increase the number of students who pay for their own schooling, thereby providing incentives and mechanisms for government to begin to redirect significant proportions of government subsidies in education to those genuinely in need of them; and (b) increase the participation of higher income groups in private, fee-paying education, thus reducing the subsidy by the non-users (generally those of lower incomes) to the users (those of higher incomes) of higher levels of education. These issues are taken up further in the final chapter, when the model for development is explained in detail.

Gender equity

Finally, it is worth remarking on another equity issue of increasing concern on a global scale, that of gender equality. The IFC case studies and country studies indicate that in this respect private education has a beneficial effect, in that private educational institutions cater for male and female students in more equal numbers than do public ones (IFC, 1998). This may reflect a higher priority accorded to girls' education amongst the higher social classes and castes, but is nevertheless highly significant in a world where the economic and social benefits of female education are known to be major factors in the overall process of development.

Company-level issues

We turn now to issues operating at the company and/or institutional level which have explicit implications for any discussion of equity. For not only are many of the education businesses examined in the previous chapter concerned with profitability and educational efficacy but they are also concerned with issues which can be seen to have a bearing on equity or social justice. A commitment to student loans and scholarships, cross-subsidisation, seeking mutually beneficial relationships with the public sector, and social responsibility programmes, are all indications of their potential impact.

Company student loans

The existence of company student loan schemes is of great significance – particularly in terms of the model of public–private partnerships developed in the final chapter – for three reasons.

First, because they encourage individual responsibility and the overcoming of dependency – students do not feel that they are owed education or training, only that they are being offered the privilege of partaking in it, that it has costs as well as benefits, and that through receiving higher wages they will be able to repay their debt, hence allowing others also to benefit from more education.

Second, they seem to overcome one of the major problems of government student loan schemes, that of default (see Barr and Crawford, 1996). Within the company loans, there is an 'honour' system working, whereby students feel indebted to the company, and would not wish to cheat it – or a future tranche of students – out of its rightful funds.

Third, it is indicated by the management of the loan schemes that their models are either potentially or actually self-financing, and, indeed, generating a surplus. This suggests an implication for their role in the wider development process, discussed in Chapter 5 below.

We found *three current student loan* schemes in operation in our case studies: TECSUP, Peru; NIIT, India; and Universidad de Los Andes, Colombia (although several educational companies, including Educor and Speciss College, had operated schemes in the past and were looking to revive these); details of the first two are given here. We were also informed from the country studies that similar schemes were operating in Romania, where loans are offered by individual universities with preferential interest rates that can cover the tuition for at most one academic year, to be repaid in up to five years, and in Turkey.

TECSUP's student credit

Most of the TECSUP core programme students come from low or middle-low income levels of Peruvian society: 54 per cent have family income below US$500 per month, 38 per cent have income between US$500 and US$1,000, and only 8 per cent have family income over US$1,000 per month. This is clearly facilitated by the presence of the loan scheme, by which anyone who passes the entrance examination is guaranteed a place on the course. All those who pass the exam are asked for details of parental income. Those who are too poor to pay the lowest rate of fee, after further checks and parental interviews, are offered credits varying from 25 per cent to 100 per cent of fees, depending on income. TECSUP issues detailed regulations, running to eight pages, for deciding on the level of credit to be awarded.

The credit is given by public deed, and two guarantors sign. In the event of non-payment, these guarantors would be approached, and legal action would ultimately be taken. But this has never yet occurred, because of the way the loans are structured, and the 'honour' system which emerges because of it. Instead of interest on repayments, the amount to be repaid is linked to the level of student fees *currently charged*. Suppose course fees were $200 per month when the student studied, but when the time comes to repay, the same course fee is $260 per month. Then $260 per month is the amount owing. The principle is that students have been given the opportunity to study for one month, so now they can give some-one else that same opportunity. If they do not repay their loan, they can see very practically that they are depriving someone else of the same opportunities which they had been given by the company. This fact, which will have been stressed to the recipients of the loans throughout their course, avoids loan defaulters.

After students finish their three-year course, they are allowed six months before they start paying back their loan. Clearly, if inflation is high, then the effective interest rate is high, and vice versa. In fact, fees have increased in the last few years by about 10 per cent per year to keep abreast of inflation. Students are expected to have paid 42 per cent of the payment by the time six years has passed.

Non-payment of the loans is avoided in part through the normal selection process: TECSUP tries to ensure that its intake will be serious students, who will then be more likely to obtain employment after graduation. However, there have been problems of non-payment of loans from about ten to twenty students in total (only a couple each year). TECSUP attempts to reschedule debts to allow them to pay back some part of their loan. It is suggested that the non-payers are only those who genuinely cannot find employment: the 'honour system' around TECSUP graduates is strong, and would inhibit people from deliberately avoiding payment. This has implications for the way other student loan schemes could be designed to avoid the problem of default.

Two people manage the loan scheme, including the Administrative Director. The costs of the scheme are absorbed in general administration, so they are not accounted for separately. Although the loan scheme started with a donation of $400,000 from the Inter-American Development Bank (IDB), the account is now in surplus, and the management argue that had this instead been a loan, rather than a donation, it would have been possible to pay back the loan and still have the system viable.

NIIT's Total Freedom Scholarship

NIIT have just introduced what they call the Total Freedom Scholarship, to celebrate India's 50th anniversary. Each year it has funded scholarships for bright students from poor backgrounds. This scheme, however, NIIT hopes will be transformed into something more. The intention is to demonstrate to other companies a working model of a student loan system which could be replicated, and perhaps for some other company to take it over and extend its application. Students are selected using aptitude tests and two interviews, to find capable but poor applicants. They are then given a loan for tuition for a one-year compressed course (instead of taking the normal two years), followed by a one-year placement with an IT company (the personnel officer of which is normally one of the original interviewers). While working on the placement, the company, in addition to paying a small stipend to the student, pays back the loan to NIIT, including interest at current bank rates, in full.

Universidad de Los Andes loan fund

The university has created a Scholarship and Loan Fund to enable students from lower socio-economic groups to attend. Loans are offered through the fund at low interest to cover the difference between the enrolment fee and the student's capacity to pay.

Currently 410 students (a little over 5 per cent of the under-graduate population) benefit from this fund.

Cross-subsidisation

Another way in which the education businesses surveyed con-tributed to the education of the disadvantaged included the prac-tice of cross-subsidisation.

In the Brazilian chains of schools, for example (Pitágoras, COC, Objetivo, Radial), and in TECSUP (Peru), it is normal prac-tice for there to be a cheaper course offered in an afternoon and/or evening shift. All on the morning course would pay full fees. But the facilities and tuition were avowedly the same in all three shifts, and hence it was apparent that the morning shift was to a certain extent subsidising the later shifts.

TECSUP's short course programme – aimed at employees and executives already in work, usually financed by companies – also charges fees which create a large surplus. This is then used in part to subsidise the 'core' programme, that is, young people taking their diplomas which will lead to work.

A fine example of cross-subsidy for less wealthy students is the Varkey Group, based in the United Arab Emirates – although this company was not a case study for the project. This group provides education to 26,000 school age students from the Indian subcon-tinent, whose parents in the main are guest workers in the Emi-rates, where state education is not available to non-citizens. The Varkey schools charge fees ranging from $50 per month to sums in excess of ten times that amount. This means that virtually all the guest worker parents can afford an education for their children, the poorest being subsidised by the better off.

Another model of cross-subsidy was offered by DPS, India, with their village schools in deprived areas. They are run at a loss by the company, using surplus from their core and satellite schools. In addition, when upgrading facilities at the core and satellite schools, old equipment is passed on to the village schools. For example, computer education facilities such as XTs and 386 machines had become obsolete in the city schools, but are far ahead of anything yet available in the rural areas.

Public–private partnerships

In addition to offering cross-subsidisation of places, several of the private education companies were playing a significant role in the public education sector, through management and quality control contracts. These companies have been explicitly contracted by the national or state governments to assist with public education, because of the perceived inadequacies of the public system, and the perceived high quality of the private alternative. Examples included the following:

- Pitágoras, Brazil, has recently entered into agreements with other big business and the Ministry of Education in Minas Gerais to introduce aspects of its quality control programme into the public sector. This involves seconding staff to work on quality control within the public schools, and advising on curriculum and management. The aim is eventually to move towards Pitágoras taking over the management altogether of particularly disadvantaged schools, receiving the normal per capita funding from government. Moreover, in 1994, the Bogota education authorities (Colombia) have contracted

Pitágoras TEC – Pitágoras's TQM programme – to help raise standards in 76 public schools.

- DPS, India, has 32 satellite schools, located in 11 states, which have been set up and owned by public sector (government) undertakings (PSUs). The DPS Society manages these schools on the government's behalf, under a management contract which specifies desired standards. These schools receive all the benefits of being part of the DPS system, and are subject to its curriculum and quality control procedures. Also, DPS runs a school in Nepal, under a bilateral agreement between the governments of Nepal and India, and a memorandum of agreement will shortly be signed for a similar management contract with a school in Indonesia.

- Federacion Nacional de Cafeteros, Colombia, manages schools in contract with the public authorities and, usually, other business investors. About 30 per cent of the funding generally comes from government – in terms of per capita funds for each student – which is then supplemented by donations from the company. The government authorities allow the company full rein to run the schools in terms of its innovative curriculum programme.

Social responsibility programmes

Finally, many of the educational companies and institutions surveyed are actively involved in social responsibility programmes. Some key examples are as follows:

- DPS, India, and its village schools programme. Government schools in the deprived area of Mewat have been taken over and upgraded, subsidised using surplus resources of the larger core schools. A similar scheme is now beginning operation in the Punjab.

- Educor has a 'black empowerment' partner, Nozala Investments, a women's economic empowerment organisation. Nozala has a right to acquire up to 10 per cent of Educor's shares, and has one seat on the Educor board and one seat on each of its subsidiary boards.

- Objetivo/UNIP, Brazil, has several social responsibility programmes. The dentistry departments in UNIP offer a free service to ordinary people in São Paulo, who can make an appointment and be used as 'models' for the final year students. Similarly, the law departments all offer free advisory services for the community. The 'nature schools' in Manaus, Angra Dos Reis, and Natal show urban Brazilians aspects of the environment and the difficulties faced by rural people. They also give advice to fishermen about environmental preservation.

- Pitágoras, Brazil, has three key aspects to its social responsibility programme. The first is 'Projeto Viver', which is aimed at enabling teenage students to engage in volunteer social work in their communities. The second, and perhaps most significant in terms of impact (and also in terms of brand promotion), is 'Projeto Pitágoras-JB'. This involves the distribution of a free newspaper, in partnership with the *Jornal do Brasil*, to 150,000 students across Brazil. The newspaper includes news stories of national, international, economic, scientific and cultural significance, as well as sports news. The project also has the financial support of Fiat. It began in September 1997 with monthly circulation, and the aim is that eventually it will be circulated free of charge in every school in Brazil, weekly. Third, Pitágoras has teamed up with *Eurocentres* – a company with headquarters in Zurich which runs language schools in Europe – to form *Eurocentres Pitágoras*. These centres are based in Pitágoras schools and offer English and Spanish lessons to students, teachers, parents and workers, all free of charge.

- NIST, Thailand, has a strong programme of social responsibility, in part from its affiliation with the United Nations and in part due to the requirements of the International Baccalaureate programme. The school provides programmes for the students to become involved with less advantaged students in Bangkok and in the countryside. The school has developed a relationship with a poor school in Thailand's economically stressed northeastern region near the Cambodian border. NIST students have travelled to the school to meet the students and to teach English and conservation of the environment. Students work on community and environmental issues in Bangkok. They also assist in fund-raising and information campaigns on such issues as the plight of international refugees.
- Trisakti University, Indonesia, has an extensive social responsibility programme – although in part this is mandated by government regulation. Activities include a mobile dental unit and a mobile medical unit which service the community free of charge. The Faculty of Law also provides law consultancy to the public.

Summary

This chapter has argued that the traditional picture of private education in developing countries as élitist is misguided. Private education businesses, it was suggested, are providing courses that cater for a wide range of socio-economic groups, including some of the poorest groups in society. To serve these groups, the businesses ensure that they are innovative and quality-conscious, as discussed in earlier chapters, thus helping to promote the future employability of disadvantaged customers. Moreover, many of the businesses are also concerned with ways in which the disadvantaged can be assisted, through scholarships, loans, cross-subsidisation and innovative public–private partnerships. At the level of businesses themselves, private education begins to take on a new perspective.

These are also macro level considerations. First, there are costs – sometimes hidden – to the public of state education and, particularly at the secondary level, the differences in costs between public and private education may not be that severe. Second, it has been argued that public spending on education in developing countries is frequently inequitable. Paradoxically, the most privileged classes seem to benefit most of all from state subsidy, even if the rhetoric of development is the opposite.

The picture emerging at both macro and micro level therefore lends support to the proposition that private education could help promote, rather than undermine, equitable development.

For the purposes of the final chapter and policy proposals, two developments are worth highlighting here. The first concerns the existence of the company student loan schemes, which have the potential to serve as a model for further developments to aid equity: many students are unable to gain access to private education because of lack of funds currently, even though their potential future earnings, had they been able to access private education, would be adequate to repay their fees. If student loans are available, this cycle of disadvantage can be overcome. The second points to the ways in which some private education companies have entered into partnership with public authorities – both at home and overseas – explicitly because it was argued that the private sector could offer a better service for the disadvantaged. Again, if this type of arrangement could be replicated elsewhere, the potential to aid development would be enhanced.

Before drawing out policy proposals, we turn to factors at the macro (country) level which affect private education.

4 REGULATION AND INVESTMENT CLIMATE

The 'snapshot' of private education in developing countries is now beginning to take shape. We have seen the existence of private education companies, and how they can be innovative and enterprising. We have also suggested that the presence of the private education sector does not necessarily exacerbate inequity. In this chapter we explore factors at the macro level which impinge upon the private education sector in developing countries, in particular concerning the regulatory regime.

I first outline the extent and nature of the private education sector in selected countries, before pointing to factors which affect the sector, particularly involving government activity in investment and regulations. All the country evidence is gleaned from the country studies conducted for the IFC study, which covered the IFC's five geographical areas, and were countries considered likely to be sympathetic to private investment in education. The twelve countries were:

- Argentina
- Brazil
- Colombia
- Côte d'Ivoire
- South Africa
- India

- Thailand
- Indonesia
- Russia
- Romania
- Jordan
- Turkey.

For these twelve countries information was gathered on those factors which influence private education sector investments, using existing datasets where possible, supplemented by interviews with key personnel in government, international agencies and education businesses.[1] The following six factors are of relevance here:

- Size of the potential market and 'maturity' of the existing private education market
- Regulatory environment
- Investment climate
- Resource availability
- Student funding possibilities
- Size and 'maturity' of the private education market.

First, it is worth noting that in all the countries surveyed there was a huge potential market for private education. In

---

1   The study was conducted before the current financial crises in Asia and Russia. Although it is hoped that the general findings will not in the medium to long term be unduly affected by these events, some caution in interpreting the comments applicable to Indonesia, Thailand and Russia, and any other countries influenced by these events, would not go amiss. The case studies of educational institutions also provided information on countries other than those in this list of twelve – for example, we gleaned information on Zimbabwe and Peru, discussed in this chapter, from the case studies of Speciss and TECSUP respectively.

many of the countries, there was express dissatisfaction with existing public schools, or inadequate provision in rural areas, and hence potentially untapped markets for private education at all levels – primary, secondary and tertiary (both academic and vocational). There were also extensive waiting lists for some of the private education establishments. It is clear that the size of the potential market would not in itself be an issue which would lead one to look unfavourably at any of the countries studied.

The second dimension of analysis concerned what we defined as the 'maturity' of the existing private education sector. This focuses on the size of the existing private education market, and its innovativeness and profitability. Our research found in the great majority of countries a large private education sector, of varying size at different educational levels. Some examples of notable private sectors include:

- Colombia: 28 per cent of total enrolment in kindergarten, primary and secondary education in the private sector increasing to 40 per cent at secondary school level
- Argentina: 30 per cent of secondary school enrolment in the private sector
- Côte d'Ivoire: 57 per cent of secondary school enrolment in the private sector
- India: 17 per cent of all kindergarten, primary and secondary schools in the private sector
- Indonesia: 23 per cent of primary and secondary school students, and a massive 94 per cent of higher education students, in the private sector.

The lowest proportions were found in South Africa, with 2.5 per cent of primary and secondary pupils in private education, and significantly less than 1 per cent in Romania and Russia. However, these figures obscure the much larger private sectors in major cities – and also of course must be interpreted in the light of the illegality of private education in the last two countries until very recently. In Guateng province, South Africa, which includes Johannesburg and Pretoria, 11 per cent of primary and secondary students are in the private sector; in Moscow, the figure is 7 per cent (about the same as in the United Kingdom).

The extent to which the private education sector was innovative – particularly in terms of providing high quality education, utilising information and communications technology, and being profitable – was of interest in the twelve countries studied. We identified many instances of extensive innovation, including growth of large school chains, vertically integrated education systems, application of innovative technology and teaching and learning systems, and use of distance learning.

We give examples to illustrate some of these themes with respect to the twelve countries examined.

Argentina

The private sector is large, with roughly 25 per cent of educational institutions in the private sector. Unlike in neighbouring Brazil, large chains of schools are not present, although a few chains have started to emerge in the last couple of years. One of these is Vaneduc, a chain that owns eight different educational sites in Buenos Aires, four of them covering kindergarten to university education. Others include one headed by the university

Universitas Inmaculada Concepción in downtown Buenos Aires, Escuela General Belgrano in the Belgrano neighbourhood, Granaderos in the Flores neighbourhood and Martin y Omar in San Isidro. All of these have grown by buying up existing schools, and it is predicted that their example will be replicated in the coming years.

None of these chains has yet extended its operations outside Buenos Aires, although if their comparative advantage is managerial expertise they may do that in the future, even if costs of control may be higher.

Outside 'formal' education, there is also a tremendous amount of educational activity performed exclusively by the private sector. Almost all of them are organised as for-profit ventures, and they offer educational services in such fields as computer training, music, secretarial work, foreign languages, support to 'formal' education (particularly at the secondary and university levels), arts and design, hairdressing, car driving, and technical jobs in electricity, motor repair and carpentry. Among these there are a number of 'chains', covering not only Buenos Aires and its suburbs but the whole country. There is no prejudice against the profit motive in these activities, maybe because they are considered more 'training' or even 'businesses' or 'shops' than education. Some of them are even becoming franchises. A few of the larger ones with regional or nation-wide coverage include:

- Academias Pitman: typewriting, computers, secretarial work, English, accounting clerk
- Academias Toil & Chat: English
- Alianza Francesa: French, tourist guide
- CIMA Profesional: accounting, taxes

- Escuela Panamericana de Arte: design
- Flego: fashion design
- Instituto Mariano Moreno: computers, secretarial work, English
- Autoescuelas Raul: car driving
- Eurovial: car driving
- Driver's: car driving
- Berlitz: languages.

Brazil

The private education sector in Brazil is remarkably innovative and successful, as the illustrations in Chapters 1 and 2 indicate. In São Paulo State, with 25 per cent of the country's population, 13.4 per cent of primary and secondary students are in private education, with the highest figure – 19.1 per cent – in high school education. The large chains of private schools operating make a significant impact on the total educational scene. These are chains of a regional and/or national nature, such as Objetivo/UNIP, Anglo, Positivo, Pitágoras and COC. The biggest is Objetivo/UNIP which has branches all over the country. Many of these chains also include universities.

Colombia

The private sector accounts for nearly 51 per cent of enrolment in pre-school (total enrolment is approximately 780,000), 19 per cent of primary schooling (total enrolment is approximately 4,855,000) and approximately 40 per cent of secondary schooling. There is an increasing trend in Colombia for private education institutions to enter into associations with foreign institutions for the development of higher education programmes. For example, the Universidad Externado de Colombia is associated with the University of Colombia in the United States, and Universidad de la Sabana. Similarly its Higher Management Programme is associated with Universidad de Inalde in Spain. The foregoing programmes offer joint degrees and the exchange of teachers and classes. They are another sign of a vigorous private education sector.

Côte d'Ivoire

In Côte d'Ivoire at pre-primary and primary level, nearly 9 per cent of schools are in the private sector, and about 12 per cent of teachers. At secondary (general) level, over 57 per cent of schools are in the private sector, and about one-third of teachers. Currently there are 20,000 students in private tertiary professional institutions, although there are no private academic tertiary institutions. The tertiary vocational sector is particularly vibrant at present, with 20 per cent of the total students taking computer-assisted management courses, and 12 per cent taking accounting and finance courses.

India

The latest survey shows that about 54 per cent of 'recognised' Indian schools were managed by government and local bodies, 39 per cent by private government-aided bodies and 6 per cent by private bodies. A very high number of schools are located in rural areas, although most of these are primary schools and only about 40 per cent are higher secondary schools. Although the number of private schools is relatively low at the primary level, it rises significantly at the secondary and higher secondary levels and includes composite schools.

There are three categories of recognised private schools: private 'unaided' schools, private government 'aided' schools and government schools. Unaided schools are privately funded and face fewer restrictions than the other two categories. At present, for instance, they enjoy the freedom to determine their own fees and admission criteria, which the other two categories cannot. A further sub-category, consequent upon the variety of religions that abound in India, are known as 'minority' schools and enjoy a certain latitude in curriculum design and operations.

A huge number of vocational institutions have also burgeoned, either independently or in joint/collaborative ventures with foreign institutions. The case of NIIT, the largest provider of computer education in India, is outstanding. The climate is presently ripe for the establishment of quality-oriented educational institutions at all levels and this is clearly evidenced by the large number of foreign institutions that are eyeing the Indian educational market and testing the waters through pilot schemes.

Indonesia

Indonesia's private education sector at the primary, secondary and tertiary levels, including vocational institutions, is extensive. While at the primary level there are only 7 per cent of children in private schools, this rises to 33 per cent for junior secondary, 54 per cent in high school and 94 per cent in higher education.

Domestic players express strong interest in developing relationships with outside investors. In fact, many such endeavours are already taking place in Indonesia, particularly with countries like Australia, the United States and Japan. A similar interest is also apparent in developing regions, which have a severe shortage of resources. Distance education is also an area where there is great demand, and especially in the outlying islands of Indonesia. With the help of the World Bank and the Asian Development Bank the central government is presently engaged in providing some distance learning opportunities, but they are still in the very beginning phases and again lack the necessary funding for expansion on either a quality or quantity basis.

Jordan

The proportion of students in the private school sector increased from 10 per cent in 1994 to 14 per cent of the total school population in 1996. There were 22,641 students enrolled in community colleges in 1995–96, more than half of them in private colleges. Private universities, the first of which started operation in 1990, are growing in number and capacity. The number of students enrolled in public universities in 1994–95 was 48,900 and in private universities 16,100.

There are currently 308 private schools registered in Jordan providing over 3,500 classrooms and catering for approximately 105,000 students. There are twelve private universities. There are also several chains of private schools operating. Over fifteen companies run two-school chains; two companies – the National Rosary Monastical Society and the Al-Ourouba Schools Company – have three-school chains; the Islamic Cultural Society and the Roman Catholic Archdiocese run chains of four schools each; the

Orthodox Society for Culture and Education and Yousef Al Athem & Co. have chains of five schools each; the Latin Patriarchate a chain of six schools; and the Islamic Center Charity Association a chain of seven schools. The international Lebanese chain, International Group for Educational Services, opened the Al Shwaifat International School on the outskirts of Amman in 1997. It runs schools in London, Lebanon, Germany and the Gulf States.

Romania

For the academic year 1995–96, 25 per cent of higher education students and 12 per cent of post-high school students were in private education. However, less than 5 per cent of vocational students were in private education, and for primary and secondary education, the official figure was zero per cent privately educated. At the pre-primary level, there were 0.06 per cent in private kindergartens.

At the higher education level, there are some 'chains' of universities:

- Dimitrie Cantemir Christian University (Bucharest) has a network of branches that cover three cities: Bucharest (three faculties), Sibiu (one faculty), Cluj-Napoca (two faculties) and Timisoara (one faculty)
- Spiru Haret University has a network of branches in five cities: Bucharest, Campulung Muscel, Constanta, Craiova and Brasov
- Constantin Brancoveanu University with its headquarters in Braila had established a network of faculties covering three cities: Braila, Pitesti and Ramnicu-Valcea.

In Romania, distance learning is a relatively new concept in education, introduced for the first time two to three years ago by British consultants. Two major private education institutions provide distance learning courses. The first is the Romanian Banking Institute which has as a major partner the British Know-How Fund. The second is CODECS – the Centre for Open Distance Education for Civil Society, mentioned in Chapter 1 – which developed, in co-operation with the UK Open University Business School, a programme of distance learning for management.

Russia

In Russia, there has been a large increase in the number of private academic education institutions – from 368 in 1993 to 505 in 1995 and to 540 in 1996. In particular, the number of private primary schools increased from 112 in 1993 to 141 in 1995 and to more than 160 in 1996; the number of basis secondary schools – from 36 in 1993 to 83 in 1995 and to more than 100 in 1996; the number of complete secondary schools – from 220 in 1993 to 301 in 1995 and to about 350 in 1996. Thus, private general education institutions currently account for 0.85 per cent of the total number of state and municipal educational institutions in 1996.

At the same time the number of private educational institutions, licensed to provide education on programmes of higher-school professional education, increased from 157 in 1994 (statistics have been collected since 1994) to 296 in 1996. Such institutions accounted for 51.6 per cent of the total number of state institutions (without taking into consideration branches and other local departments). At primary school level, the figure is 4.2 per cent and at secondary level 1.2 per cent of total students are in private education. As noted earlier, this relatively low figure obscures the fact that in Moscow itself about 7 per cent of all primary and secondary students are in the private sector.

Private universities can be considered as a major factor contributing to the expansion of continuing education. Many private higher schools give opportunity to many people, especially the unemployed and military officers transferred to the reserve, to receive higher education or re-training in a reasonably short period of time. There are a number of federal and local programmes to re-train the unemployed and military transferred to the reserve.

South Africa

Interestingly, one of the most innovative private education sectors is also one of the smallest. In South Africa, private schools account for only about 2.5 per cent of the total number of students (1 to 2 per cent at primary level and 3 to 4 per cent at secondary level), although, as noted, this national figure obscures the much larger concentration in Gauteng province, where about 11 per cent of all primary and secondary students are in private education.

However, there are key players in South Africa which show the for-profit sector in very innovative form, viz., Educor and ADv-TECH, as noted above in Chapter 1. Damelin College High School has played a path-breaking role in changing the nature of private schooling in South Africa and making for-profit schooling 're-spectable'. Damelin was being imitated before the formation of the growing Educor Group, quoted on the Johannesburg Stock Exchange, but the obvious success of Educor has drawn greater attention to education as a potential area of private investment. The company ADvTech was recently listed on the Stock Exchange and is on a similar take-over trail to that pursued by Educor over the past few years. The Association of Private Colleges of South Africa (APCSA) has more than 120 members offering a range of courses, including business, travel/hotel, marketing/sales, public relations, human resources, secretarial, bookkeeping, legal, reception/ switchboard, computer applications, graphic arts/advertising, interior decorating/architecture, paramedical and ABET/literacy.

There are no degree-awarding private universities in South Africa yet – Educor delivers courses for the state correspondence university, UNISA – but a draft Higher Education Bill which is currently under discussion does make provision for the registration of private higher education institutions in future.

Thailand

It is striking that vocational education growth in the private sector in the period 1993–96 exceeded that in the public sector (80 per cent private versus 44 per cent public). The demand for education catering for children of the middle classes is typically met by private institutions in the academic stream and those focusing on vocational courses leading to a certificate or diploma. These students continue their education after finishing the lower secondary level. As for future expansion, there seems to be a growing demand for private distance learning: thus the National Technological University (NTU), based in Fort Collins, Colorado, USA, has already set up an agency in Thailand. Most clients are corporate and most courses are in technology. There is also a vigorously increasing demand for tutoring. Many private tutoring institutions are appearing and they offer courses tailoring especially for entrance exams for students wanting to enter secondary schools and universities both in public and private schools. Most tutors are from prestigious schools and universities. One particularly strong growth sector in the tutoring market is education in languages. There are already hundreds of private tutoring schools offering short courses in foreign languages.

Turkey

In the past fifteen years both the demand for, and the supply of, Turkish private schools has exploded. The number of schools increased almost five-fold and the student capacity four-fold between 1981 and 1995. The structural changes and the liberalisation of the economy caused rapid urbanisation and a rapid increase in the wealth of the upper classes who are more likely to seek private education for their children. On the supply side, the government eased the regulations on private education and promoted private enterprise as in the rest of the economy.

The rapid changes in and the liberalisation of the economy during the 1980s and 1990s have put private education institutions on top of the political agenda. Growing demand has led many investors to open private schools. By a change in the Law of Higher Education in 1992, it was made easier for non-profit foundations to establish private universities.

However, private schools are not utilised to full capacity. According to official figures, in 1995–96 the capacity utilisation of private schools in Turkey was a mere 57 per cent. (Total capacity being 319,099 and the number of students enrolled in private schools 182,352.) On the other hand, some prestigious private schools have always had waiting lists and an excess demand for places. In 1997, out of the 21,395 students who participated in the private high school examinations, 6,230 were admitted directly to a private high school and 1,697 were on waiting lists.

The target of the government is to increase the current ratio of private school students in general primary and secondary education from the current 1.5 per cent to 6 per cent in the short term and 15 per cent in the long term, throughout the country.

The competition within Turkey will be fierce in the two big cities. Istanbul and Ankara have most of the private universities and private high schools. There will be increasing demand for private education in the coming years, in the fast developing provinces of Izmir, Bursa, Denizli, Gaziantep, Izmit, Eskisehir and Adana. Some investors have already been investing in private schools in these regions and demand is very high.

Regulatory environment

The biggest stumbling block for private education in many countries may be the regulatory environment. This could severely inhibit the potential for private education to contribute to development. Although regulations may be intended to protect consumers and maintain standards, they often act to inhibit and, in some cases, stifle needed educational opportunities which the private sector could otherwise provide. There appear to be three ways in which regulatory regimes can inhibit private educational growth and investment:

- Regulations are substantial, but mainly ignored; however, the threat of enforcing them inhibits and threatens operations
- Regulations are applied in an arbitrary or *ad hoc* fashion

- Petty regulations are enforced, leading to inconvenience, inefficiency and a brake on growth.

Regulation in Argentina and Zimbabwe

The cases of Argentina and Zimbabwe[2] provide classic examples of these three areas, and are worth explaining in some detail, to give a flavour of the types of regulations found in many countries which inhibit development of the private education sector.

Under private schools' Regulatory Requirements in the Province of Buenos Aires (which cover the largest population), a private school must ask for authorisation from the provincial government with regard to:

- the name of the institution (art. 4)
- staff movements (art. 10)
- the limit of students per class (art. 12)
- any religious ceremony (art. 18)
- any text in a foreign language. Two copies of a translation must be submitted to the ministry 'in letter-size paper written only one side, signed by the director in each page. Any change in the text must follow the same procedures' (art. 28).

Moreover, the following also apply:

- All ceremonies are regulated down to the smallest detail. It is regulated how students will stand at a ceremony, who will

---

2   Information for Zimbabwe was obtained from the case study of Speciss College – Zimbabwe was not one of the country studies.

direct it, who will raise the national flag, when the national anthem will be sung (art. 20)

- Time schedules will be the same as government schools and any change must be authorised by the ministry (art. 30)
- Only books and texts approved by the provincial ministry of education will be used (art. 15).

The Regulatory Requirement for Secondary Schools comes with such specific instructions as (and there are many more):

- Any professor doing a scientific experiment must register it in a specific register
- If a professor gives a lecture at the school, the text of it must be submitted beforehand in written form and filed at the school (art. 57)
- Assistants to teachers must keep a book with all practical classes given, stating the instruments and materials used. This book will be signed by the director every month (art. 58)
- Administrative personnel cannot converse about subjects different from their office duties once work-time has started (art. 69)
- Any sport activity must be approved by the authority. The request for approval must state the organising institution, the kind of exercises or gymnastics tests that will be carried out as well as the exhibition by-laws which must be approved by the authority (art. 172).

Similarly, in Zimbabwe, many of the most onerous of the regulations are simply ignored by the various ministries involved (Education, Higher Education, and Manpower Planning and

Development). For example, under the regulations, a for-profit college has to seek the relevant ministry's clearance for *each* member of staff employed, and for *every* fee increase and *every* change to, or supplement to, the curriculum offered. In many educational settings, each year, extensive management resources are engaged writing to the relevant ministry seeking permission for fee increases and new members of staff, and proposing new curriculum options. These communications are seldom answered, and the assumption is that they are simply ignored. However, this brings uncertainty, and would inhibit investment, because a change of heart by a government which wanted to hinder private education could be effected simply by enforcing existing legislation. At the present time, such a change of policy seems unlikely, as the government in Zimbabwe recognises that private education is a necessary route to development; however, this is not to say that such changes could not occur, and the fearful atmosphere that developed around private education in 1980 could return.

The key point is that in both these countries – and many similar ones – most of these regulations are not followed, nor even controlled. However, this brings us to the second category, of regulations applied in an arbitrary or *ad hoc* manner. For example, in Argentina, private schools get periodic reviews from inspectors requesting them to comply with any of these or many other regulations. They may be punished for not following them to the letter, which keeps the directors in apprehension of the arrival of the inspectorate. This certainly has a bureaucratic cost, and would be of particular concern if an institution was seeking outside investment.

Similarly, in Zimbabwe, the rather arbitrary way in which regulations are enforced – and even new ones apparently invented – is shown by what took place when Speciss bought the Academy of Learning[3] franchise for Harare. Speciss tried to register this as a new college under the Manpower Planning Regulations, but was told that this could only be done if the government's qualifications were offered. Not only was this against the ethos of the Academy of Learning, which offers its own qualifications, but, more importantly, it is *not* stipulated in the appropriate Zimbabwean regulations, seemingly invented in an *ad hoc* way to inhibit the expansion of Speciss. Eventually, an ally from within the Ministry of Education pointed out that if it was announced that the Academy of Learning franchise was an integral part of Speciss College, there would be no need for separate registration! This was the route eventually followed. Again, this not uncommon kind of incident shows the difficulties of working under regimes with strict regulation of private education.

Regulations which are of the third type – that is, regulations which are regularly enforced, and which undermine the initiative of private education at the primary and secondary school level – include the following in Argentina:

- The mandatory national curriculum. This restricts the ability of private schools to compete through the content of the curriculum or the methodology of education.
- Provisional registration and accreditation of private educational institutions, with the threat of withdrawal of recognition of education delivered. At the primary and secondary level, education is regulated by procedures which

---

3   This is a South African franchise, now operating world-wide and owned by Educor.

only grant a provisional accreditation at the beginning of the process, with final accreditation given after evaluation of its performance. If this accreditation is denied, all education given in the meantime will not be recognised. This imposes a severe barrier to entry, making it very difficult to attract students at the start of operations.

- The Teachers' Statute. This regulates the labour contract for all teachers both in the public and private sector. It grants all teachers 'stability' as long as the teacher maintains good conduct. He/she cannot be fired, nor transferred or suspended without due process. All teachers are paid according to years of service. This prevents private schools from implementing what they deem to be sensible systems of incentives for good performance, since pay is tied to seniority and not to performance and productivity. Teachers also enjoy several kinds of paid leave which include not only a 30-day vacation per year but also long periods for sickness or maternity and up to six months a year to study. According to recent research, a comparison of average days worked in a year gives 220.7 days for a worker under the general labour contract law but only 118.5 for a worker under the Teachers' Statute. This generous system requires private schools to have more than one teacher on the payroll to obtain the services of a full-time teacher in the classroom.

- In private universities, contracts with professors are regulated by general labour laws affecting any other job. This brings a specific problem to all universities, state or privately owned. Most of the professors at Argentine universities are part-time, having other commitments apart from their academic work. Regulations request universities to have them contracted as 'employees', therefore with all the payroll taxes that both employee and employer need to pay. This is not only very costly for the universities, it is also unfair to the professors since, for example, those who are already employees in their main activity are forced to register as independent professionals and start a second monthly payment to social security, even if they only teach a few hours of classes each month.

Similarly, in Zimbabwe, there is a range of relatively minor additional regulations which are regularly enforced in practice, which inhibit the growth of private education in various ways. These include the following:

- Marketing in schools is forbidden
- Planning zoning regulations inhibit growth
- Import duties lead to expensive text books and computer equipment
- Study permits require considerable staff time and expense in order to recruit foreign students – in the Chitepo EFL department there is a full-time post employed for one day a week obtaining study permits
- Employment of expatriate staff is extremely difficult, even in shortage subject areas.

Regulation in other countries

The situations in Argentina and Zimbabwe are not unusual. In other countries similar regulations, particularly of the third type, impede the work of private educational institutions.

Brazil

When a new course is inaugurated at the university level, 'a team of bureaucrats from Brasilia invade'; it prescribes exactly how many books there must be in the library, how many classrooms and laboratories must be used, the space made available in these, how many qualified teachers are needed, etc. Such conditions must be met in order to have the course approved. Given changing technology, sometimes these conditions seem rather archaic. However, they have to be followed even where they make no educational sense, wasting time and resources. Student numbers at the university are also controlled by the Ministry of Education, and any proposal for increasing them has to be approved. Currently it takes approximately one year for a university course to be approved – this is a substantial improvement over the five years that was common until recently.

India

There have been rumblings about fee control for private schools, which may erupt into action by the state governments to limit fees and fee increases. Recently, in Delhi, the courts were petitioned to restrict fee hikes proposed by schools, to meet the added burden resulting from the recommendations of the 5th Pay Commission, which has proposed hefty wage increases for teachers. In their interim order the judges permitted private unaided schools to raise their fees by a maximum of 40 per cent, to meet their additional emoluments bill.

Indonesia

At the tertiary level, institutions are allowed a limit of up to 40 per cent 'local content'. The other 60 per cent of the curriculum for private education institutions is designed by the Centre for Curriculum Development (CDC). Local content is, however, also subject to government approval. All private universities must submit a development plan every two years for Ministry Curriculum Approval. For-profit institutions are illegal, as are surpluses. However, it is common practice for private education institutions to retain up to 50 per cent of their surplus on an annual basis. As this is an illegal practice, it leads to bribery being common.

Russia

The government has been very strict in controlling private universities, closing many of them ostensibly because of mismanagement, lack of suitable professors and inappropriate educational standards. The Russian government is controlling any further expansion by setting very strict standards for accreditation.

Turkey

For-profit higher education is also illegal. It is reported that some private university proprietors disguise profits through, for example, inflated personal salaries and creative accounting, and thereby evade this injunction, but this again leads to bribery and corruption. There are very detailed regulations relating to higher education which are frequently revised. Keeping up with the regulations and revisions is a major preoccupation of university administrators, and lengthy guidebooks are published privately to help with the process. Private universities are not required to comply with the regulations, but if they fail to do so then they will not receive accreditation, their students will not be able to defer military service and their graduates' degrees may not be recognised by employers. Amongst other things, the regulations provide for the teaching of Turkish language and history to all undergraduate students and lay down detailed criteria for the grading and promotion of academic staff.

Investment climate

A related issue concerns the investment climate in the country, our third dimension of analysis. Of particular impact will be government receptiveness to private investment in education.

In the various countries studied there was a very broad range of factors affecting the investment climate for education. In most cases, private investment in education is feasible, including external financing and foreign investment. However, in most countries, local capital market activities in this sector were very limited, and in many cases – for instance, India, Argentina, Indonesia and Romania – there were barriers to for-profit educational institutions. In some countries, such as Jordan, Indonesia, Côte d'Ivoire and Thailand, there is a government-led effort to encourage investment in certain sectors of private education as a means of alleviating capacity constraints. In many cases the investment climate is more favourable (more open investment, foreign investment, allowance of for-profit companies) for higher levels of education (particularly for technical subjects) and vocational education (for example, in Romania, Turkey, Thailand and India).

Government receptiveness

The climate facing potential investors is determined largely by the willingness of national governments to tolerate or encourage a major role for the private sector in the provision of education. Four dimensions are worth distinguishing:

- the principle of private (non-government) provision
- the acceptability of foreign investment
- the issue of profit-making from education, and
- the differing applicability of these factors at different levels of education.

First, in the twelve countries studied there is increasing acceptance of private provision, albeit with varying degrees of enthusiasm. In some countries (for example, Argentina), there is more encouragement of community financing, religious schooling and other NGO involvement than of commercial provision of education, but in all countries the non-government sector is gaining ground both in size and in acceptability. In Thailand, Colombia, South Africa and Argentina, for example, the ratio of private to public even at the primary education level is increasing.

By far the clearest evidence for the expansion of private and foreign-based education is in the tertiary sector. For example, the vocational private school enrolment in Thailand has been increasing at a significantly greater rate than that in the public sector, with the private sector enrolment rate of the fifteen to seventeen year old cohort now being 50 per cent of the total. In higher education, meanwhile, there are now 36 registered private universities or colleges. In Colombia over two-thirds of higher education institutions are currently in the private sector while in Indonesia the figure is more than nine-tenths.

Second, government receptiveness towards private provision does not necessarily extend to *foreign* investment. Some countries (such as Turkey) which encourage private schooling are averse to foreign involvement, usually for nationalistic or religious reasons. As a general rule it seems that governments are more hospitable to foreign investors when the investment concerns tertiary education, education that includes professional training and instruction in subjects that have a mathematical, statistical or scientific content.

Third, in many of the countries studied, for-profit education companies were not tolerated. India, Romania and Turkey, for example, encourage private financing of schools and universities but only on a non-profit basis.

Fourth, each of these aspects of government receptiveness may apply differently at different levels of the educational system. Several countries (for example, Romania and Turkey) concentrate *public* investment on the age range of compulsory education, and *private* investment is encouraged mainly at pre-school level and at post-compulsory level, in vocational training and higher education. Foreign investment is often directed towards the top end of the system (for example, in Romania and Thailand) where foreign languages are more widely taught and used, and where international perspectives and practices are particularly appreciated. In some countries (for example, India) for-profit education providers tend to be restricted to short-term vocational training courses (such as computer skills training, driving lessons) which are directly related to income-earning opportunities in the labour market, and the more long-term general education of young people is still largely provided on a non-profit basis in order to protect it from becoming too narrow and specialised by commercial or competitive pressures.

The receptiveness of national governments to private, foreign and for-profit investment in education is reflected in the pronouncements of politicians and in policy documents, and is sometimes embodied as fundamental clauses in national constitutions (as in India, for example). These determine the overall investment climate, but at a more practical level, it is the precise legal requirements and formal regulations with which potential investors have to be familiar and to which we now turn.

Resource availability

The fourth dimension of analysis concerns the availability of resources for expanding the private sector. This overlaps with other dimensions here, including at its simplest level the willingness of parents to pay for their children's schooling, or students to pay for their own, the availability of student loans and subsidies, and of potential providers of capital investment in private institutions – discussed under separate headings. The country studies strongly suggest that encouragement of private investment and its growth in recent years have increased total investment in education in many countries. They indicate that the private sector in education has mobilised additional resources both for recurrent expenditure and for capital investment in education, and therefore enabled a channelling of a greater proportion of national income into the educational system as a whole.

This dimension also includes the availability of other resources, such as water, electricity and availability of land or buildings to lease and buy, the absence of which would severely limit the investment opportunities in private education. It also includes more advanced technology, such as telecommunications, satellite and Internet networks, which are essential for many of the more innovative educational companies.

In many of the countries surveyed, none of these was a problem. In Brazil, for example, there are no indications that the absence of any of these factors would be an obstruction for investment in new private schools. In Russia, infrastructure suitable for the creation of private secondary and higher schools (water, electricity and telephone communications) is available in virtually all towns. However, in some regions there are interruptions of heat and electricity supply.

In some countries, however, there were greater problems with available infrastructure. In Romania, for example, the availability of utilities is variable, even in large cities. The availability of such infrastructure is reflected in the price of land. The most problematic are, in some areas, gas and terrestrial phone lines. Requests for phone line installations are sometimes 20 years old! If a person or institution is in a hurry the only solution is to pay some 'extra costs' directly into the pockets of bureaucrats who can approve such requests – a phenomenon found in many other countries, such as Zimbabwe and India.

In several countries the availability of suitable land for the construction of buildings and/or campus sites, especially at an affordable price, would be a severe stumbling block for new private education facilities. Within Indonesia's urban areas, for example, such land is limited and expensive. There is more land available in the rural areas; in these areas, however, access to adequate infrastructure is limited. In Russia, one of the principal obstacles to the expansion of the private sector infrastructure is the high price of land and buildings and high cost of renting. It is necessary to bear in mind that premises to be bought or rented must comply with sanitary, hygienic and construction norms, which very rarely is the case. As a rule, newly established private schools rent vacant premises that belong to state and municipal schools, kindergartens, state technical secondary schools and higher schools. In Romania, land for building in major cities is widely available but at high prices. For instance, in Bucharest prices may vary between $100 and $700 per square metre. To that must be added construction costs of at least $300 per square metre. By contrast, properties to buy suitable for education purposes are not numerous and therefore the prices they command are very high. The Ministry of Education owns many educational facilities that are now vacant owing to the reduction of activities in post high-school and vocational education. These facilities are sometimes rented to private institutions but at market prices. Other facilities available for rent are the premises used in the past for social activities by the large socialist enterprises (which now are privatised, liquidated or restructured), such as clubs and residential accommodation. Usually these premises are in very bad condition, necessitating further investment in renovation. In Côte d'Ivoire, the price of land is seen as a major factor in limiting expansion of the private sector, and in keeping fees high. This is particularly the case in Abidjan.

Another issue raised is that in several countries foreign investors are unable to own or even lease land. In Indonesia, foreign investors are not allowed to purchase land although they can lease for a fixed period of time. In Jordan, restrictions on land use have now been lifted except for some areas (for example, the Dead Sea) and some sectors (mining). According to the Investment Promotion Corporation, anyone can now buy and own land in Jordan, although for non-Jordanians the approval of the Prime Minister's office is required. It is said that this is a simple, straightforward procedure.

In South Africa and Zimbabwe, a distinct problem may arise for potential investors in certain areas. The usage of land in tribal areas is controlled by Tribal Authorities. There is common ownership by the tribe and no private ownership. Members of the tribe obtain the right to use allocations of land, almost in perpetuity, subject to the rights passing to members of the family. The building of a school on tribal land would require the allocation of a piece of land by the Tribal Authority, but would not confer title to the property.

Finally under this heading, it must be noted that in a small minority of the countries surveyed governments themselves offer aid to private universities, for capital and current expenditures.

In Turkey, state aid is granted to private universities, for education, research, library, investment and other current expenditures. The maximum aid is determined to be 45 per cent of the university's budgeted expenditures. In the academic year 1997–98 TL 6,500 billion was granted (including to Turkish universities abroad such as Hoca Ahmet Yesevi University in Kazakhstan and Manas University in Kirghiz Republic). Baskent University and Bilkent University will be granted TL 1,750 billion each (US$8.75 million).

In Thailand, government also provides financial support for private higher institution in the following ways:

- *Revolving Fund* for the Development of Private Higher
  Education Institutions. This fund was established in April
  1990 to provide loans at 4 per cent interest for private higher

education institutions for purchasing instructional materials, equipment and facility construction. The amount of the fund is 500 million baht (US$20 million) for ten years (1990–2000). In 1994, the fund reached 240 million baht. The ceiling for each school loan is limited to 30 million baht for construction and 10 million baht for purchasing instructional materials. Very few higher private institutions have so far applied for this fund because of the limited loan ceiling and amount of paperwork required.

- *Specific Assistance and General Subsidies.* Each year, the government allocates an additional amount of 5.5 million baht for expenses in the academic and administrative development of private higher education institutions, categorised as follows:
  - Research Development Fund: 700,000 baht/year
  - Academic Development Fund for such projects as composing, translating or compiling texts: 300,000 baht/year
  - Administration and Faculty Development Fund: 500,000 baht/year
  - Community Service and Volunteer Work Camp Fund: 4,000,000 baht/year.
- *Human Resource Development Loan Fund.* In March 1995, the administration of then Prime Minister Chuan Leekpai set up a low-interest loan fund of 20,000 million baht to support private education. A total of 10,000 million was allocated for commodity and construction loans for private institutions offering courses in the fields where there were shortages of human resources. This fund covered institutions at the secondary, vocational and higher education levels. Another

7,000 million baht was set aside for commodity and construction loans for institutions offering courses in general fields. The rest of the 3,000 million baht fund was earmarked for student loans, discussed below. The Private Education Institution Support Committee was established to specify criteria for provision of financial support to existing and new private education and occupational training institutes. Institutions meeting certain conditions were eligible to apply for fixed assets loans. These loans had a repayment period of not more than fifteen years, with grace periods of not more than five years.

Student funding possibilities

The final dimension of analysis of opportunities for private education concerns the availability of student funding. In the majority of countries surveyed, students and/or parents paying fees accounted for the greatest proportion of fees paid for private education. However, in half of the countries surveyed, there were some government subsidies to private education, either funding to the schools to provide teacher salaries, or on a per capita basis – either allocated according to particular 'deserving' students, or to particular schools deemed worthy by government.

In Argentina, for example, 37 per cent of private schools (2,816 schools, figures from 1994) receive what is called 'total' subsidy from the government, that is, they receive a subsidy which amounts to the total cost of teachers' salaries plus payroll taxes; 29 per cent (2,191 schools) receive a 'partial' subsidy covering only a percentage of such costs; the remainder receive no subsidy at all. Such subsidies do not cover capital expenses. Note that this subsidy is directed to the schools themselves, and is not allocated on a per capita basis related to pupil numbers.

In Côte d'Ivoire, the government pays scholarships for deserving students to attend private schools. The scholarship for such students is fixed at 120,000 CFA francs for lower secondary and 140,000 CFA francs for upper secondary. At primary level, the figures are 30,000 CFA francs for schools where fees are below 50,000 CFA francs, and 27,000 CFA francs for those whose fees are 50,000 CFA francs or higher. Such scholarships paid to private schools totalled 9 per cent of the 1997 government budget for the education and training sector.

In South Africa, the practice of subsidising private schools, which the Province of Natal had done for many years, was extended to the rest of the country in 1986. Government subsidies to private schools in Gauteng make up a relatively insignificant proportion of the total education budget but represent an important source of income for the schools. Presently, the Province of Gauteng grants 25 per cent and 50 per cent subsidies (based on the per capita cost of government schooling) to approved private schools, the differentiation being based on the quality of schooling being provided by the schools as measured by matriculation results. However, the present subsidies received by private schools do not necessarily translate into lower school fees because some of the schools, fearing the possible summary withdrawal of the subsidies (as is presently threatened), prefer to devote the subsidies to upgrading the buildings and other school facilities, whilst maintaining their fees at the level necessary to cover all running costs. Out of a total government education budget of R25,120 million in 1996–97, R225.4 million, or about 1 per cent, was budgeted for private schools as these state subsidies. It must be noted that Educor, the case study discussed in Chapters 1 and 2, does not receive such state subsidies for its high schools, as it is registered as a company rather than an educational institution.

In Thailand, there are three levels of subsidy to private schools: 40 per cent, 60 per cent and 100 per cent of the amount set by the government as the 'standard individual educational expense', that is, per capita cost in government schools. In general, schools receiving subsidies were set up before 1974. Since then the government has ruled against providing subsidies to any additional private schools, arguing that such schools should be self-supporting. Those schools receiving the 100 per cent subsidy are usually connected with charitable or religious foundations. Schools receiving the other rates are generally owned by private companies or individuals. The total annual subsidy granted for private schools has increased from 366.7 million baht in 1977 to 3,602.8 million baht in 1997.

In Turkey, government student scholarships and loans exist throughout the education system. In pre-higher formal education in 1997–98, less than 1 per cent (91,044 students) are given government scholarships. Monthly scholarship amounts were TL 678,000 in January 1996 and TL 1,020,000 (US$10.8 and US$12.3 per month respectively at the current exchange rates). Government scholarships in higher education cover more students than in primary and secondary education. In 1997, 222,411 university students (30 per cent of all formal education university students) received tuition loans and 170,766 received education loans. The amount of scholarships in October 1997 was TL 6,000,000 for undergraduate students, TL 12,000,000 for Master students and TL 18,000,000 for PhD students (around US$35, US$70 and US$105 if converted at the exchange rates of the time). The number of scholarship recipients doubled from 1986 to 1997. There are many other government and public institutions giving scholarships to students. Foundations, non-governmental and non-profit organisations, state economic enterprises, companies, schools, universities, some local administrations (for example, Istanbul municipality) are all donors of scholarships and/or education loans. However, the number and the amount of such scholarships are estimated to be rather low. Finally, private educational institutions are required by law to give scholarships to their students: 2 per cent of private high school students and 10 per cent of the foundation university students are required to be admitted without payment for tuition.

Finally, in Colombia, government funds particular private schools in exact proportion to enrolment. There is modest but growing evidence of similar funding in other developing countries not surveyed here, such as Bangladesh, Belize, Chile, Dominican Republic, Guatemala, Lesotho and Pakistan (West, 1997).

Two comments can be made about the viability of such forms of funding private education.

First, an *a priori* argument can be made against state subsidies of private schools which are not on the basis of per capita funding. If private schools are simply given subsidies whatever their intake, then this would seem to encourage – or at least not discourage – inefficiencies, because there would be little incentive for such schools to attract their customers by offering high educational standards. If research demonstrated that such subsidies did lead to inefficiencies, then this would be an argument against the efficacy of some of the subsidies currently on offer to private education. However, it would not rule out the per capita funding, which, as West (1997) has pointed out, is akin in many ways to voucher schemes.

Second, in our case studies we came across some companies which would have been able to receive state subsidies for their schools, but which did not seek them. Speciss College, Zimbabwe, and Educor, South Africa, were two examples here. The impression given was that accepting the subsidies would bring in a whole gamut of additional regulation, and it was considered that being subject to these was simply not worth the extra funds. Indeed, one of the suggestions was that the extensive regulation of private education in some countries was in part because of the need to ensure accountability of the public subsidies, and that if over-regulation was to be avoided, then perhaps losing these subsidies was a necessary price to pay.

If these comments were to be generalisable with further research, then this might well suggest the undesirability of any such public subsidy to private education. We cannot go so far at present, however, and some suggestions about this kind of subsidy will be taken up in the final chapter.

In most of the countries surveyed, there were no government student loan companies, and banks were not usually in the habit of lending to students either, with the following exceptions:

- In Jordan, the Housing Bank has a student loan programme with 9 per cent (inclusive) interest rate. There must be an account for five years with the bank. The amount of the loan depends on the amount in the account and collateral.
- In Romania, some commercial banks have introduced a new system of cards and accounts for students of some public universities. In these accounts the students can receive their

scholarships, and a student can be credited with a maximum amount of Lei 150,000 (approximately US\$20), that is, the average monthly level of a scholarship provided by the state. This is an experiment designed by the commercial banks to accustom the students to using credit cards and modern payment systems.

• In South Africa, commercial banks offer student loans for university study. Typically they cover only part (70 per cent) of a student's fees. The loans are repayable after completion of studies and interest rates are lower than prime rates. According to the Association of Private Colleges of South Africa, the banks do not make loans available to their students.

Finally, in some countries, private associations are attempting to move into student loans. In Côte d'Ivoire, there are no private student loan companies, and banks do not get involved in financing private education. Recently, however, a women's association was set up to try and find funds for self-paying students in universities and private schools. It is too early to assess the outcome of this project.

As far as government student loan programmes were concerned, we came across three examples in our country studies, only one of which was of any current significance. In Indonesia, the government had introduced a system of student loans in 1984. However, they did little to ease financing burdens or improve equity. Commercial banks lacked the mechanism for loan collection. Meanwhile the rate of default was very high and the fund became 'non-revolving'. The result was the cancellation by the banks of student loan schemes. In the Russian Federation, the Federal Law on Education (p. 6, Art. 42) provides for the creation of a special mechanism of providing loans for students in secondary vocational schools and higher professional schools. However, until now the government has not identified the terms and procedures for such crediting. Finally, and the only significant current example, in Thailand there is a student loan scheme, which provides many interesting lessons for discussion.

Thailand's student loan scheme[4]

In March 1995 the Thailand government established a low-interest Human Resource Development Loan Fund of 10 billion baht ($1=31.81, as of 31 July 1997). Seven billion of this is allocated for commodity and construction loans for institutions, while three billion baht is set aside for student loans. This loan covers all educational expenses including tuition fees and personal educational expenses. The fund is jointly managed by the Ministry of Finance (MOF), the Ministry of Education (MOE) and the Ministry of University Affairs (MUA). It began to operate in May 1996. The fund is available for low-income students at high school level (both vocational and general stream), as well as students in higher education within the country. Of the total amount, 1,200 million baht was allocated to MUA and 1,800 million to MOE. Students at private educational institution are also eligible for the loans.

The ceilings for loans are various according to level of education. They are:

- for continuation in secondary school (secondary 4, 5 and 6, in

---

4   This section is based on West and Tooley (1998).

academic and vocational streams): not exceeding 62,500 baht
* for junior college level: not exceeding 70,240 baht
* for university: not exceeding 100,000 baht.

Although the initial impression is that the above described loan system is a sober attempt at self-financing, a little extra scrutiny raises several questions. First, little regard seems to have been paid to the world experience of the serious problem of student loan defaulting, a problem that has probably not fully asserted itself yet in Thailand because of the newness of its loan programme.

Second, there seems to be a failure to recognise how substantially the loans are subsidised. The student's payment of interest, for instance, starts two years after the completion of the degree. Since his/her course takes at least three years, the total interest free period is five years at minimum. The true cost to taxpayers of providing these loans, meanwhile, is the cost of interest foregone by them over the five years in question. Alternatively the true cost is the real borrowing rate faced by government when it raises on the capital market the funds made available (via loans) to students. This latter amount, of course, is ultimately payable by taxpayers. Remembering that this burden will be shared by low-income families who do not participate in higher education, the problem of inequity is seriously magnified or aggravated.

The largest concealed subsidy, however, arises because, when the student borrower is eventually obliged to pay interest, it will be at the unrealistic rate of only 1 per cent per year! Assuming levels of inflation greater than 1 per cent (which is well justified) this implies a *negative* real rate of interest (that is, another subsidy). It is no wonder that the number of students in Thailand seeking a loan jumped to 400,000 in 1997, from 131 in 1996.

The issue of student loans is worthy of further general comments in view of widespread misunderstanding of the subject. Most countries with loan schemes offer students credit in the form of a 'mortgage' loan, defined as one wherein repayment is made over a relatively short specified period, usually with fixed monthly payments. Interest rates and the maximum length of repayment are used to calculate the fixed periodic payments. At the same time, students who borrow to help pay for their education face risky outcomes since the future value of a degree is not immediately apparent and the risk is probably greatest for students from poorer backgrounds insofar as their future job and earnings prospects are less favourable. For them the obligation to pay fixed future repayments commits the debtor to repay an open-ended proportion of his/her income. Mortgage loans may therefore often deter access among the very groups loans are intended to reach.

To help meet these equity and efficiency problems, three developed countries – Australia, New Zealand and Sweden – have established *income-contingent* loan systems under which the debtor is not committed to repay an open-ended proportion of his/her future income. Instead, the loan is repaid as a predetermined fixed percentage of post-graduation income above a certain threshold. Income-contingent loans thus limit the extent of debt burdens in a given year and substantially extend the repayment period. For these reasons the barriers to lower-income students are significantly reduced. Despite these advantages there is no evidence so far of the adoption of the income contingency version of loans, and the model introduced in Thailand is no example of it.

Countries with fairly long experience of student loans of the mortgage type have found that the default problem looms large. Because students borrowing under conventional short-term fixed-rate (mortgage-type) loan plans are unable automatically to spread their indebtedness over a long period, and so cushion the irregularity of their income payments in the early years, many of them are tempted to default. The usual income-contingency programme, in contrast, can be expected to have much lower defaults because it embraces long and flexible periods of repayment. The information requirements, however, are substantial. It is here that the coupling with the income tax process becomes crucial since the revenue authority possesses data on the current location and income status of individuals far superior to that which can be assembled by any single company or bank. These institutions will invariably confront the problem of 'moral hazard' where many student borrowers disappear without trace.

A World Bank Report (World Bank, 1991) has indeed confirmed that experience shows reliance on tax departments to be 'far less costly to administer'. In developing countries the income tax machinery is likely to be at present too primitive to handle all the necessary tasks.

The phenomenon of 'moral hazard' in student lending is usually a positive function of the size of the student population. Such considerations make it easier to explain our discovery of the three current student loan schemes in operation described in Chapter 2 above, viz., in TECSUP, Peru, NIIT, India and Universidad de Los Andes, Colombia. These are not attempts at national student lending, but are all confined to relatively small student communities wherein, as suggested above, it is relatively easy to instil co-operative behaviour. As we stated, the 'honour system' around TECSUP graduates is strong, and would inhibit people from deliberately avoiding payment. All these observations lead us to predict that the latter small scale student loan schemes will have a greater chance of survival than the government operated national loan scheme recently launched in Thailand.

Conclusions

This chapter has discussed various macro factors which affect the private education sector in developing countries. Building on the evidence amassed for the IFC study by in-country consultants (IFC, 1998), the extent and nature of the private sector in many countries was first set out. It was noted that in all of the countries surveyed, there are likely untapped markets for private education – expressed in terms of dissatisfaction with public schools, waiting lists for existing schools and inadequate state provision, particularly in rural areas. The huge size of many of the private education markets is also apparent – putting the small size of the market in the UK into perspective. In many of the countries surveyed, we also pointed to the existence of the types of chains of schools and education companies discussed in earlier chapters. We moved on to examine the ways in which governments impede or help the private sector. First, we illustrated two particular examples of regulatory regimes which contained many factors likely to impede the development of private education. The imposition of substantial regulations, applied in an arbitrary or *ad hoc* fashion, or the imposition of petty regulations, results in inconvenience, inefficiency and a brake on growth and investment. But these inefficiencies could well affect the potential for private education companies to expand and cater for the less affluent, and increase educational opportunities for the middle classes. However, it is also clear that there are some governments in developing countries which see it as their role to support private education, through subsidies to students and/or schools. In part, indeed, it may be the very presence of these subsidies which has led to the heavy regulation in the first place, to ensure accountability of public funds. Some of these models of public funding of private education are taken further and considered in the final chapter policy proposals.

After examining some resource constraints and government receptiveness to investment in private schools, we explored various other constraints on the private sector, including the availability of resources, and student funding possibilities. The issue of student loans is a live issue in developing countries. The problem of access to higher education in particular can potentially be alleviated if suitable models of student loans can be developed. One particularly sophisticated and advanced student loan scheme was found in Thailand, which created the potential for poor students to have access not only to university education but also to high school education. However, the scheme had the manifest disadvantage that it was not an income-contingent loan, but a mortgage type loan, and hence would be likely to suffer from the problem of repayments default. It also represented a huge subsidy to those who would have access to higher education, which, given the regressive taxation system, would likely mean inequity in distribution of higher education.

Given these considerations, we now turn to some tentative policy proposals, drawing together the ideas from the paper to create a possible model for equitable development involving the private sector in education.

5   CONCLUSIONS AND
POLICY PROPOSALS

This monograph has pointed to the extent and nature of the burgeoning private education sector in developing countries, based on the findings of the IFC's study of investment opportunities in private education (IFC, 1998). Far from confirming the common stereotype of a relatively few expensive schools, catering only for the élite, we revealed a richly innovative and entrepreneurial sector in many countries, catering to a wide spectrum of demand and tailoring courses for almost the whole socio-economic range. In particular, we provided a snapshot of a relatively unknown aspect of the sector – the private education company. We aimed to give case studies of these companies, to give an impressionistic view of this sector, with details of their history and background. We then showed how such companies viewed their success, focusing on the factors which were seen as important to key personnel within the company, and to students and staff within them, such as product and process innovation, the security of a strong brand name, expansion using a variety of franchising methods and strict quality control procedures.

The private education company is of particular interest, it was argued, because it seemed to have the potential to counter some of the more common objections to private education, viz., that there will be an information problem, and that government would be needed in order to promote investment in research and development and quality control. It was suggested that private education companies could overcome both of these issues.

We also explored the common conception that promoting private education would necessarily exacerbate inequality. When a variety of factors at the macro and micro level was taken into account, it was suggested that promoting private education had the potential to do the opposite. In part this argument is based on factors at the country level, showing the inequity of public education funding, and the costs, sometimes hidden, of public education. In part it was based on the ways in which many education companies and institutions had their own methods, sometimes *ad hoc*, sometimes formalised, of subsidising poorer students.

Finally, the monograph pointed to factors at the macro level, which could impede or enhance the potential of the private education sector. Examples of the ways in which regulatory regimes impinge on private education were examined, and ways in which student funding possibilities were being enhanced in some countries were explored, in particular concerning the ways in which they could increase access for the disadvantaged.

The tentative nature of many of the conclusions should be stressed. The IFC study sought to describe a sector which was little known, in particular to describe it from the point of view of the viability of investment in it. Thus case studies were opportunistically selected which revealed facets of the educational market that had not been previously examined; these were looked at in the context of countries selected as likely to be more favourable than others to investment in private education.

Given this context, it is clear that we cannot generalise from these findings without further research – and the study has highlighted many areas of interest for further study and exploration.

However, rather than leave the issues there, until further study has been conducted to make generalisations possible, we conclude with some tentative policy suggestions based on the findings thus far.

These policy proposals must be taken in the following spirit: *if* the impressionistic snapshot of the private sector conveyed in Chapters 1 and 2 can be shown to hold more generally than for the small number of companies and institutions surveyed; and *if* the equity considerations sketched in Chapter 3 can be reinforced by further exploration; and *if* the extent of the regulatory regimes and the student funding possibilities outlined in Chapter 4 fit in with a broader picture; *then* the following policy proposals would emerge as being favourable to help promote equitable development through private education in developing countries.

Some might feel that formulating these policy proposals is putting the cart before the horse, and that results of further studies should be available before anyone endeavours to consider possible policy proposals arising from them. On the contrary, I suggest that these policy proposals, tentative as they are, can serve to motivate further research and debate, and to provide one context for that debate to take place.

Finally, before moving to the policy proposals, the following context needs to be noted. The author of this monograph has mooted ideas elsewhere (Tooley, 1996), building in part on the seminal works of Peacock and Wiseman (1964), West (1965), Friedman (1955), and others, which develop the notion that there is a justified role for the state in education in terms of ensuring a safety net for those whose parents are too poor or too irresponsible to provide educational opportunities for them. This could be in terms of funding and regulation, but it was unlikely to be in terms of provision. The onus was then on government, and the apologists for government intervention, to justify any greater intervention than these, to show how it clearly met educational needs and opportunities better than market suppliers. The suggestion was always that government intervention excluded or pushed out private suppliers, and that these had incentives and accountability structures which were better able to ensure quality than the public sector.

Clearly, these ideas were developed in the context of theoretical reflection on education in developed countries – in particular, the USA and the UK. One challenge of this particular study has been to see if similar ideas relate to the context of education policy in and for developing countries. The conclusion of this paper – offered in the tentative spirit noted above – is that a broadly similar perspective on the respective roles of the public and private sectors in developing countries might be highly beneficial. If our goal is to ensure high quality educational opportunities for all in developing countries, then the way forward may be to base this on the same principles. Government intervention – in terms of funding and regulation – could be there to ensure that there is a safety net for the disadvantaged. But it need not be assumed that government intervention should be there to subsidise those who do not need subsidising, nor that government intervention should be allowed to crowd out – through over-regulation and unnecessary supply – the private sector which could otherwise provide vibrant educational opportunities if permitted to do so. The proposals, then, are not about privatisation, but about ways in which this 'mixed economy' of public–private partnership in education can be extended.

Given these cautionary caveats, I suggest that a 'modest

proposal' (with apologies to Jonathan Swift) emerges, which embodies the recognition that there already exist in many countries informal mechanisms for sharing the burden of education development between the public and private sectors. Making these mechanisms explicit and encouraging their adaptation and adoption in other countries could lead, it is suggested, to rather optimistic prognosis for development.

It is worth spelling out the argument supporting this policy proposal, as developed throughout this paper, in the form of five propositions.

1. In many developing countries, educational entrepreneurs are able to satisfy demand, by creating educational opportunities which satisfy the following criteria:
- they are profitable (or make a surplus)
- they are financed totally (or almost totally) from student fee income
- they charge comparatively modest fees, and hence are accessible to many socio-economic groups, not just the élite. *(Chapters 1 and 2)*.

2. Such entrepreneurs have often created education companies which run chains of schools, colleges and universities, sometimes on a franchise basis. These educational chains benefit from economies of scale, invest in research and development, provide consumers with the informational benefits of brand names and take risks to provide for 'risky' (often the disadvantaged) customers. They overcome many of the objections to private education, and hence provide the

basis for the model of public–private partnerships to aid development. *(Chapters 1 and 2)*

3. But is not private education inequitable? Some considerations suggest not – viz., the inequity of public provision, the hidden costs of state education, and a discussion of the way some private education companies respond to the needs of the disadvantaged, by provision of innovative social responsibility programmes, subsidised places and student loan schemes. *(Chapter 3)*

4. If private education is to be able to assist in development, then factors at the macro level, in particular the regulatory environment, need to be conducive to their functioning. However, in many countries, current regulatory regimes inhibit investment and expansion of the private education sector. *(Chapter 4)*

5. The suggested model of public–private partnership in education which could potentially enhance equitable development, based on the discussion of propositions 1–4, has the following five dimensions:
   - Policy-makers and opinion-formers need to be informed of the development potential of the types of education companies discussed here, and their implications for equity.
   - Investment from organisations such as the IFC in private education projects, which satisfy conditions of profitability, educational efficacy and social responsibility, should be encouraged.
   - The regulatory environment in countries needs to be

modified to ensure that such companies can emerge and prosper, in order to play their full role in equitable development.

- Links between education companies and institutions and the public sector, similar to the ones found in several countries, should be encouraged, to enable the management expertise, incentive structures and investment potential of the private sector to inform, challenge and potentially 're-engineer' the public sector.
- The sources of finance available to allow students – and, in particular, disadvantaged student – to benefit from private educational opportunities should be extended. This could involve at least the following: (a) facilitating the setting up of company student loan schemes, perhaps aided by overseas investment from bodies such as the IFC. This may be in terms of a global student loan company, channelling funds through education companies, and financed through international investment; (b) extending voucher schemes and other per capita subsidy funding of private education by governments.

A modest proposal

The 'modest proposal' aims to describe mechanisms which:

- extend the range of private educational opportunities offered
- liberalise regulatory regimes
- bring into public education the perceived management and investment superiority of the private sector, and
- extend the range of finance available to allow students to enter private education.

The purpose of this section is to show ways in which those who are at the sharp end of education policy in developing countries – including those who finance development loans – can be made more aware of the relative merits of investment in, and encouragement of, the private sector, and how these two aspects will support development. Although demand for private education is extremely high in all the countries surveyed, and although the quality of private educational opportunities is perceived in general as being far higher than those on offer in the public sector, clearly many are inhibited from finding private education because of the level of fees charged. Even though this is not as serious an objection as many would feel to private education, it is nonetheless still an issue for many people. The modest proposal suggests two ways of overcoming this problem, by allowing the channelling of existing public funds into private education companies, and by encouraging the development of company student loan schemes and voucher or similar per capita funding systems by government.

Informing policy-makers

Firstly, many in policy-making circles in developing countries are likely to be apprehensive about the potential links with private enterprise in education in order to move the development agenda forward. Part of the process must be in persuading such people that there are tremendous opportunities for the private sector, and that it need not offend equity by promoting it. Some of the arguments in this text may be useful for this purpose, and conferences and seminars would need to be arranged to this end.

Changing the hearts of policy-makers is one step. But private education could be further enhanced by encouraging greater investment.

Encouraging investment

Concerning the encouragement of investments, international organisations such as the IFC have a clear role to play here. Such organisations are likely only to have a mandate to consider projects which are financially and educationally viable, and considerations of equity would also come into any decisions. Likely candidates for investment are already emerging, which are worth outlining to give a flavour of likely developments:

Financing of new campuses

Several companies would like to build and develop new campuses, but cannot afford in-country interest rates and/or cannot find sufficient new equity. Companies in Africa, Latin America and central and eastern Europe gave information about their expansion plans along these lines in confidence to the author.

Finance for franchises

A theme emerging in several countries is that a useful source of investment would be for those companies operating franchise systems to allow the franchisees to borrow money to finance the initial building and furnishing of premises, or to expand their campuses as demand increases. These funds would be credit lines to the franchisees; the risks of investment would be low, given the success of the companies which operate franchises. For example,

NIIT in India currently has 400 franchises, and only three or four of these have failed as businesses over the last ten years. It is seeking to open many more in the next two years, and has indicated that it would welcome this type of investment. Similarly, Educor in South Africa has a very strong record with its franchises. Such possibilities offer great potential for investment aimed at small-scale projects. Moreover, as already noted, they have the additional advantage of not only enhancing educational development, but also of developing entrepreneurial talent at the grass roots as new entrepreneurs are encouraged into education by the existence of sufficient seed money for their activities.

Finance of 'south-south' investment

Several of the companies studied are expanding, or seeking to expand, into other developing countries. Such expansion could be assisted greatly by debt or equity finance. For example, from our case studies we found:

- Damelin (Educor, South Africa) has opened franchises over the last two years in Namibia, Botswana, Malawi and Lesotho, and is likely to be interested in further expansion into other neighbouring countries.
- NIIT has opened centres and franchises in eighteen countries, including China, Indonesia, Malaysia, Zimbabwe and Singapore. In each of these countries, they are seeking the development of many franchises.

Finance for 'the technological imperative'

Many of the companies and institutions examined are creating opportunities with new technology which could easily be used to enhance both profitability and equity. For example, TECSUP is seeking funding for its Satellite Tuition System. Under this model, the mining companies in various regions of Peru would buy satellite teaching facilities for their workers. But once the facilities are in place, the companies could easily, if they wished, allow them to be used, either free, or very cheaply, by local people, perhaps as a PR measure. Hence the poor as well as the companies could benefit, yet the investment could be very profitable.

Finance for a revolving loan fund

Although we have suggested a loan fund particularly for franchisees of successful known education companies, it is also worth considering the possibility of a loan fund making investment available in local currency for any educational concern. Such a loan fund would be riskier than the franchise model suggested, and would need extremely careful vetting of applicants; nonetheless it offers a potentially very useful mechanism for investment aimed at small-scale ventures.

These are just some of the possibilities which emerge for encouraging investment in private education in developing countries. Such investment could also be enhanced by consideration of the regulatory regimes within the countries involved.

Regulatory changes

Concerning changes to the regulatory environments, organisations such as the World Bank could play a key role here in passing recommendations to relevant countries, in order to enhance the educational and developmental viability of their private education sectors. It is clear that the regulatory regimes in many countries, although perhaps intending to protect consumers and ensure quality educational provision, act to inhibit and in some cases stifle needed educational opportunities which the private sector could otherwise provide. From the IFC study, four general ideas have emerged, which could form the basis of recommendations to governments interested in extending educational opportunity by this route:

First, the political uncertainty of many regulatory environments is likely to turn investors away. There are many regulations in place which are not enforced; however, if they were, then investment in private education would become untenable. Or there are regulations which are enforced in an *ad hoc* way, again extremely worrying to investors. The examples given of Argentina and Zimbabwe in Chapter 4 – which we suggest are likely to characterise similar regimes elsewhere – graphically illustrate this problem.

Second, many countries have regulations against for-profit private education (for example, Argentina, Jordan, Russia, Turkey), or which restrict the amount of profit which can be returned to investors (for example, Thailand). This could have a debilitating impact on investment and growth of the private sector, and it would be useful if these regulations could be reviewed or adapted – particularly in the light of the discussion above which suggests that there may be nothing to fear and plenty to gain, in terms of equity and investment in educational innovation, from allowing for-profit companies to play their part.

Third, in some liberal regimes, regulations are emerging which may have the effect of severely inhibiting private education. South Africa is an example. Such countries appear to be following the Anglo-Saxon model of a highly regulated qualification regime, initiated in Scotland, followed by England and Wales, New Zealand and Australia. Many in private education are in favour of these reforms, but this endorsement should be treated with caution. It may be simply a case of existing private education providers seeking useful barriers to entry for competitors.

Fourth, at the simplest level, there are many regulations which inhibit the private education sector, and which could be repealed. For example, in Peru, import duty is charged on donated machinery, while in Zimbabwe, import duty is charged on textbooks. Similarly, it is very difficult for skilled expatriate staff to obtain work permits in some countries, thus inhibiting growth in certain areas (such as India or Zimbabwe).

These are general ideas for regulatory changes, and of course the specifics would have to take into account the particular situations in each country. Interestingly, there are developments in the regulatory regimes in some developing countries which give cause for some optimism. For example, the law on for-profit education was liberalised in Peru two years ago. The government went this route for two reasons. First, because it wanted the possibility of international companies entering the education market. Second, because it wanted mining companies and other industries which were already operating in the rural areas to start schools in these areas of greatest need. Although neither has happened at the time of writing, it is significant that at least one developing country government has explicitly sought to encourage the development potential of for-profit education.

In combination, these first three components of the 'modest proposal' – the informing of policy-makers, the encouragement of investment, and some regulatory changes – would seem to have the potential for advancing educational development. They sit comfortably with many processes which are currently under way in developing countries, and point to ways in which such processes could be enhanced. Moreover, in the spirit of our tentative conclusions – which need further research to support them more strongly – pursuing these three proposals would allow empirical cases to develop which would further help us understand the potential role that the private education sector has in promoting equitable development.

However, several of the examples found in this paper suggest the possibility for further developments which could more radically enhance the education system in developing countries. These, the fourth and fifth elements of our 'modest proposal', are spelled out in more detail.

Encouraging public–private links

In the global study, we saw examples of small but nonetheless significant public–private partnerships involving some of the education companies. Examples such as DPS satellite schools, Pitágoras' involvement with management and quality control in Minas Gerais schools and in Colombia, and the Colombian Coffee Growers' Federation model of partnership, all offer a potential model for others to follow. Each was introduced because of the perceived inadequacies of the state sector, and the perceived advantages which the private sector could bring. These models seem to offer a significant potential way forward for enhancing the management and financial expertise in the public sector. The keys to these developments seem to be three-fold:

- the management contract between the public authorities and the private companies
- the willingness of the public authorities to fund the schools (at least in part), while allowing the private sector to manage them
- the willingness of the private sector to invest in the schools in anticipation of a small return through efficiency savings, or through improved public relations.

Interestingly, there are parallel developments taking place in the UK and USA which are linking public and private sectors in a similar way. For example, in the UK, two proposals were set out in the 1998 Schools Standards and Framework Act which are of relevance here. The first is the Education Action Zone model. There is a recognition that in some relatively deprived areas public (state) schools have failed to provide quality opportunities for students. Hence, there is a proposal for action zones to be set up – initially up to 100 of these zones – which allow the possibility of private companies (including for-profit companies) to take over the management of public schools. The companies which take them over will be given only the funds which are currently devoted to public education, plus a small 'sweetener'. There is already interest from private for-profit education companies – including, interestingly, NIIT, the Indian company outlined in this paper. They see the potential for making their own investment in the public sector, following their models which have been so successful elsewhere, leading to improved schooling for the disadvantaged and with the potential for an eventual return on the investment. The second aspect of the legislation concerns individual schools which have been 'failing' (in the government's definition, involving continual low standards) for more than two years. These schools can now be taken over by central or local government, and then handed over to an education company to manage (that is, nationalised in order to be privatised). Any education company doing so would likely invest heavily in the school, including in training teachers, but would again be able to run the schools so that a small return could be made through efficiency savings. As this is being written, the first local education authority in England and Wales (the equivalent of school districts in the USA) – Surrey – has agreed to put the management of one of its failing schools out to tender, and there are three private education companies suggested as being ready to turn in bids (*Daily Telegraph*, 1998).

Similarly, in the USA, for-profit education companies such as the Edison Project and Sabis have taken over the management of charter schools and other schools from school districts, using only the funds that would normally go into public schooling, but with the aim of making an eventual profit after massive investment in the schools: in the case of Edison, on average investing US$1–$2 million in each school that is taken over. (It is of course implicit in all of these models that there is some waste and inefficiency within the public sector which could be rectified with better management.)

The examples from India, Brazil, Colombia, the UK and the USA suggest a potential way forward for public–private partnerships in education in other developing countries. Consider first the case where governments are currently putting sufficient funds into public education at school or university level, but the quality of such public education is not perceived as high, and the education system, in particular, is failing already disadvantaged students. In such cases, transferring these funds, with suitable contractual protection in case of failure to deliver quality education, to a known private education brand could revitalise public education. It could bring all the benefits of efficiency, technological innovation and quality control to bear on a previously inadequate education.

Second, in situations where governments are not able to offer sufficient funds to provide enough incentives for a private company to take over the schools, then such companies can still become involved, either by supplementing the funds available from their own resources as a social responsibility cross-subsidisation measure (as with the DPS Indian village schools), or by seeking aid or philanthropic funds to supplement them (as Edison is doing in California schools, where the per capita funds available from the state are not adequate to fund the massive investment it seeks).

If such models could be developed in some of the developing countries surveyed, it is likely that the supply-side would be extremely eager to take part, and could greatly enhance the quality of educational provision for the poor, by providing a known quality brand name education for them. Countries from this study such as South Africa, Zimbabwe, India and Brazil would seem to be examples where this could be most readily accomplished. We await further research to show other countries in similar positions.

Opening up funding possibilities

The final part of the model addresses the issue of funding from the viewpoint of the individual student. The IFC study showed at least two ways in which this was being accomplished in developing countries, student loan schemes and voucher-type schemes. Both provide the basis for further enhancing the role of the private sector.

Student loan schemes

The discussion in Chapter 4 suggested that there may be considerable disadvantages – in terms of equity and also in terms of default rates – to *country* student loan schemes, particularly in terms of mortgage-type loans, while the illustrations in Chapter 2 pointed to the potential of *company* student loan schemes to solve some of these problems. If further research backed up these suggestions, then one way forward for development would be clear – to encourage companies to develop such student loan schemes, and to seek ways of financing these.

It has been noted that the company student loan models described for TECSUP and NIIT are potentially not only self-financing in the medium term, but could also generate a surplus. Key aspects of each of these loan schemes seem to be:

- Initial substantial investment to ensure that the scheme can be set up. In the case of TECSUP this came from outside the company in the form of donations; in the case of NIIT it came from internal investment.
- Careful vetting of students who take such loans to ensure that they are serious about study, and hence will be employable after graduation. Note that this vetting does not only have to consider academic achievement to date – which may rule out some deprived children. In the case of NIIT, the company is

exploring means of identifying students with particular *aptitude* for courses, even if currently such students, because of their deprived backgrounds, have not been able to demonstrate their aptitude in terms of concrete academic achievement.

- Careful administration of the loan to ensure that an 'honour system' is brought into being. Students must feel sufficient loyalty to the company to recognise that default on the loan is out of the question, and/or that they will be depriving future students of opportunities if they do default.

- Careful mentoring of the student to help ensure he or she is able to gain employment after graduation, to help repay the loan. Companies such as NIIT and TECSUP in any case have extremely close links with potential employers; these links are deployed to assist in finding employment for graduates with loans to repay.

For companies or institutions not in the happy position which NIIT found itself in, with the ability to provide the initial investment for a loan fund, the possibility arises of this type of funding being made available from outside investors. Indeed, the possibility suggests itself of the formation of regional student loan companies – or even a global company – to provide loans while still gaining a return. Again, such a project may become a key channel for investment from sources such as the IFC. But such a loan company would have to be able, it is suggested, to fulfil the above four conditions. The success of any larger scale operation is likely only to be possible, therefore, if funding is channelled through existing educational suppliers, to ensure that student loyalty keeps default rates low.

Voucher-type schemes

The second way of channelling funding for disadvantaged students to allow them to attend private schools involves government funded voucher-type schemes or direct subsidies to private schools. We noted several examples of these in Chapter 4. The key features for viable schemes, we noted, were:

- Avoid funding schools irrespective of their student numbers – in other words, per capita funding of schools is the preferred option
- Be careful to weigh up the benefits of public subsidy of private schools with the disbenefits that excessive regulation as a result of such subsidy could cause.

Only per capita subsidy of private schools is likely to ensure that educational establishments are subject to market mechanisms to keep standards high. And if public subsidy will have to lead to excessive regulation, then it must be considered whether such subsidy would be worth these extra burdens to private education.

Lessons from the global education industry

Our modest proposal has highlighted ways in which private education in developing countries could be enhanced. With policy-makers informed of the potential of the private sector, with investment encouraged, with regulatory regimes liberalised, with private companies contracted to take over inadequate state provision, with comprehensive student loan systems or vouchers in place, the private education sector could be in a strong position to further the promotion of equitable development.

But the snapshot of the 'global education industry' also invites us to look again at public education in *developed* countries such as the UK and the USA. Perhaps there are lessons for educational provision in these countries to be drawn from this evidence? Travelling to Brazil and witnessing private education companies so willing to invest in technological innovation and curriculum development in schools set me wondering about the paucity of innovation in state schools in England. Travelling to South Africa and finding private education companies so concerned with the future destinations of their students – to the extent that they buy up recruitment companies – raised questions about the concerns of our state schools. Seeing in India companies so involved with quality control to ensure standards are high for all clients led to doubts about the lack of quality control procedures at home.

Perhaps there are lessons from the global education industry for developed as well as developing countries?

REFERENCES

Barr, Nicholas ([1987] 1993) *The Economics of the Welfare State*, Weidenfeld and Nicolson, London.

Bray, Mark (1996) *Privatisation of Secondary Education: Issues and Policy Implications*, UNESCO, Paris.

Chubb, John E. and Terry M. Moe (1990), *Politics, Markets and America's Schools*, The Brookings Institution, Washington DC.

Colclough, Christopher (1997), 'Education, Health and the Market: An Introduction', in Colclough, Christopher (ed.), *Marketising Education and Health in Developing Countries – Miracle or Mirage*, Cassell, London.

Cowan, L. Gray (1990) *Privatisation in the Developing World*, Greenwood Press: New York.

Daily Telegraph, 16 October 1998.

Friedman, Milton (1955) 'The Role of Government in Education', in Solo, Robert A. (ed.), pp. 123–44, New Brunswick, NJ, Rutgers University Press.

Gewirtz, Sharon, Ball, Stephen J., and Bowe, Richard (1995) *Markets, Choice and Equity in Education*, Open University Press, Buckingham.

Glenn, Charles L. (1995) *Educational Freedom in Eastern Europe*, Cato Institute, Washington DC.

Hanushek, Eric A. (1995) 'Interpreting Recent Research on Schooling in Developing Countries', *World Bank Research Observer*, pp. 227–46.

IFC (1995) *Privatization: Principles and Practice* (Lessons of Experience Series, Vol. 1), IFC, Washington DC.

IFC (1996) *International Finance Corporation Annual Report 1996*, IFC, Washington DC.

IFC (1998) 'Investment opportunities in private education in developing countries', Final Report, IFC, Washington DC. (Three volumes: Volume 1: Summary Report; Volume 2: Case Studies; Volume 3: Country Studies.)

IFC (1999) *Investment Opportunities in Private Education in Developing Countries: Conference Proceedings*, Washington DC.

Karmokolias, Yannis, and Maas, Jack van Lutsenburg (1997) 'The Business of Education: A new approach for the World Bank Group?', mimeo, Washington DC.

Lewin, K. M. (1987) *Foundations in Austerity: Options for Planners*, UNESCO/IIEP, Paris.

Mitra, C. R. (1998), 'The NIIT Academy: A "university in the making"', *Economic Affairs*. Vol. 18, No.3, September.

Molnar, Alex (1996) *Giving Kids the Business: the commercialization of America's Schools*, Westview Press, Boulder, Colorado.

Peacock, Alan T. and Wiseman, Jack (1964) *Education for Democrats*, Hobart Paper No. 25, Institute of Economic Affairs, London.

Perelman, Lewis (1992) *School's Out*, Avon Books, New York.

The PROBE Team (1999) *Public Report on Basic Education in India*, Oxford University Press, Oxford and New Delhi.

Tilak, Jandhyala (1997), 'Lessons from Cost-Recovery in Education', in Colclough, Christopher (ed.), *Marketising*

Education and Health in Developing Countries – Miracle or Mirage, Cassell, London.

Tooley, James (1996) *Education Without the State*, Institute of Economic Affairs, London.

Tooley, James (2000) *Reclaiming Education*, Cassell, London.

West, E. G. (1965), *Education and the State*, Institute of Economic Affairs, London.

West, E. G. (1975) *Nonpublic School Aid*, D.C. Heath, Lexington, MA.

West, E. G. (1997) 'Education vouchers in principle and practice: a survey', *The World Bank Research Observer*, 12, 1, 83–103.

West, E. G., and Tooley, J. (1998) 'Student loans in developing countries: government versus company loans', *Economic Affairs*, Vol. 18, No.3.

World Bank (1986) *Financing Education in Developing Countries*, World Bank, Washington DC.

World Bank (1991) *Discussion Paper, No. 137*.

World Bank (1994) *Higher Education: The Lessons of Experience*, World Bank, Washington DC.

World Bank (1996) *From Plan to Market: World Development Report 1996*, Oxford University Press, New York.

Ziderman, Adrian and Albrecht, Douglas (1995) *Financing Universities in Developing Countries*, Falmer Press, London.

ABOUT THE IEA

The Institute is a research and educational charity (No. CC 235 351), limited by guarantee. Its mission is to improve understanding of the fundamental institutions of a free society with particular reference to the role of markets in solving economic and social problems.

The IEA achieves its mission by:

- a high quality publishing programme
- conferences, seminars, lectures and other events
- outreach to school and college students
- brokering media introductions and appearances

The IEA, which was established in 1955 by the late Sir Antony Fisher, is an educational charity, not a political organisation. It is independent of any political party or group and does not carry on activities intended to affect support for any political party or candidate in any election or referendum, or at any other time. It is financed by sales of publications, conference fees and voluntary donations.

In addition to its main series of publications the IEA also publishes a quarterly journal, *Economic Affairs*, and has two specialist programmes – Environment and Technology, and Education.

The IEA is aided in its work by a distinguished international Academic Advisory Council and an eminent panel of Honorary Fellows. Together with other academics, they review prospective IEA publications, their comments being passed on anonymously to authors. All IEA papers are therefore subject to the same rigorous independent refereeing process as used by leading academic journals.

IEA publications enjoy widespread classroom use and course adoptions in schools and universities. They are also sold throughout the world and often translated/reprinted.

Since 1974 the IEA has helped to create a world-wide network of 100 similar institutions in over 70 countries. They are all independent but share the IEA's mission.

Views expressed in the IEA's publications are those of the authors, not those of the Institute (which has no corporate view), its Managing Trustees, Academic Advisory Council members or senior staff.

Members of the Institute's Academic Advisory Council, Honorary Fellows, Trustees and Staff are listed on the following page.

The Institute gratefully acknowledges financial support for its publications programme and other work from a generous benefaction by the late Alec and Beryl Warren.

For information about subscriptions to IEA publications, please contact:

Subscriptions
The Institute of Economic Affairs
2 Lord North Street
London SW1P 3LB

Tel: 020 7799 8900
Fax: 020 7799 2137
Website: www.iea.org.uk/books/subscribe.htm

Other papers recently published by the IEA include:

WHO, What and Why?
Transnational Government, Legitimacy and the World Health Organization
Roger Scruton
Occasional Paper 113
ISBN 0 255 36487 3

The World Turned Rightside Up
A New Trading Agenda for the Age of Globalisation
John C. Hulsman
Occasional Paper 114
ISBN 0 255 36495 4

The Representation of Business in English Literature
Introduced and edited by Arthur Pollard
Readings 53
ISBN 0 255 36491 1

Anti-Liberalism 2000
The Rise of New Millennium Collectivism
David Henderson
Occasional Paper 115
ISBN 0 255 36497 0

Capitalism, Morality and Markets
Brian Griffiths, Robert A. Sirico, Norman Barry and Frank Field
Readings 54
ISBN 0 255 36496 2

A Conversation with Harris and Seldon

Ralph Harris and Arthur Seldon
Occasional Paper 116
ISBN 0 255 36498 9

Malaria and the DDT Story

Richard Tren & Roger Bate
Occasional Paper 117
ISBN 0 255 36499 7

A Plea to Economists Who Favour Liberty: Assist the Everyman

Daniel B. Klein
Occasional Paper 118
ISBN 0 255 36501 2

Waging the War of Ideas

John Blundell
Occasional Paper 119
ISBN 0 255 36500 4

To order copies of currently available IEA papers, or to enquire about availability, please contact:

Lavis Marketing
73 Lime Walk
Oxford OX3 7AD

Tel: 01865 767575
Fax: 01865 750079
Email: orders@lavismarketing.co.uk